D0539200

Acknowledgements
We would like to thank Mr and Mrs D Mulvey for the use of their garden for the cover photograph.

Percy Thrower's First-time Gardening

Illustrations by Colin Gray, the Hayward Art Group and Tony Streek.

Hamlyn
London · New York · Sydney · Toronto

Contents

First published in 1979 by
The Hamlyn Publishing Group Limited
London · New York · Sydney · Toronto
Astronaut House, Feltham, Middlesex, England

Filmset in England by Photocomp Ltd., Birmingham
in 9 on 10pt. Monophoto Rockwell Light
Printed in Italy
ISBN 0 600 37419 X

Introduction

Acquiring a garden for the first time is an exciting experience although it can also be a bit daunting. My own first garden was a small patch under a walnut tree at the back of our cottage. Admittedly this was not the best place for a garden with the problem of shade and competition from tree roots. I did rather better with a garden at school and here I grew lettuce, radish, carrots, beetroot, beans, peas and a few flowers. And this really makes the point for me, because to keep an interest in gardening you must achieve a measure of success. Of course, there are always some failures – plants that die or seeds which fail to germinate – but if you can work out what went wrong then next time you should be able to overcome the problems. Going about things in the right way in the first place also helps to keep the problems to a minimum.

In my lifetime I have learned from my failures and in my guide to *First-time Gardening*, I have tried to offer advice which will help the new or inexperienced gardener avoid many of the common pitfalls and I hope, too, that the hints and much of the information may be of interest to those who are more knowledgeable.

All the basic gardening skills are described as well as the reasons for their use and there are sections on lawn care, improving the soil, the role of trees, shrubs and other plants and help is given on recognising and treating the common pests and diseases. In a practical subject such as gardening, clear illustrations have as much value as the words and the many drawings included here have been worked out to explain or expand the text which accompanies them.

If this book helps you to develop the basic gardening skills, and, even more important, encourages a life-long interest in this most rewarding of hobbies, I shall be very pleased.

The soil, where gardening begins

Good cultivation of the soil is the basic principle of good gardening. Unless the soil is treated correctly, the time and money spent on plants to go in it may all be wasted. When faced with either a brand new or existing garden, the first thing to do is to find out what kind of soil it contains and then, as it is much too costly to replace, you will have to make the best of it. Don't despair, even if it does become glue like in wet weather and dries to bricks in dry weather, or if it refuses to hold any water no matter how many gallons you empty on to it: all types of soil can be improved by correct treatment and all soils can be made to grow something if the plants are chosen carefully.

Soil layers

It is important to distinguish between the top 20 cm (8 in) or so of soil which is known as topsoil, and the layers beneath this which are known as subsoil. Topsoil is generally darker in colour and contains nutrients and organic matter, while subsoil contains neither the nutrients nor the bacteria necessary to break down organic matter and in many instances will not support plant life. These two layers should always be kept separate during cultivation but, unfortunately, on many newly built housing estates the subsoil is brought to the surface by the builders and the topsoil may even have been removed altogether. Subsoil requires years of good cultivation before it becomes fertile.

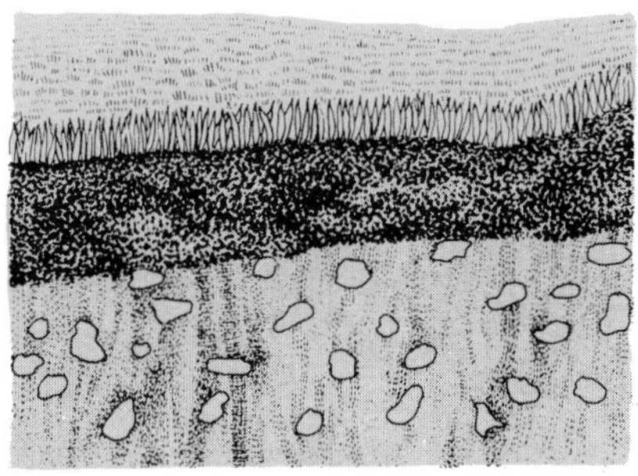

Left **Soil layers. The darker topsoil has a finer texture, the subsoil is lighter and coarser**

Soil testing

Simple soil-testing kits can be used to establish the basic nature of the soil: whether it is acid (deficient in lime) or alkaline (limy). This is an important point to know when the planting up is considered. There are more expensive kits on the market which tell you if the soil is deficient in the main nutrients – nitrogen, phosphate and potash – but, personally, I would only test for the presence or absence of lime. An even simpler way of finding out about this is by chatting to a neighbouring gardener, or by studying the plants which are already growing in the area: rhododendrons, camellias, primulas, most heathers indicate an acid soil, whilst clematis, lavender, and pinks are lime lovers.

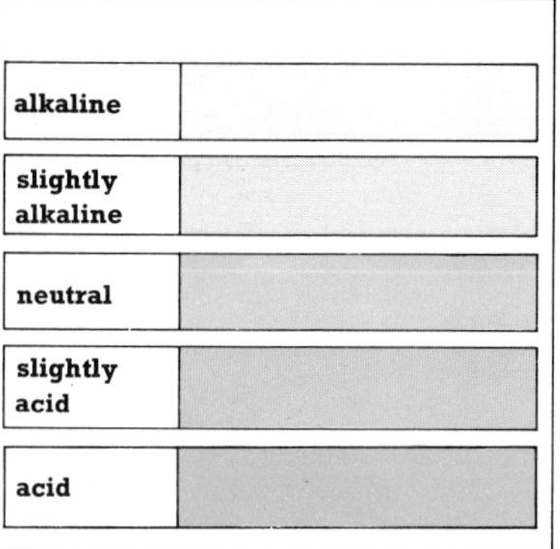

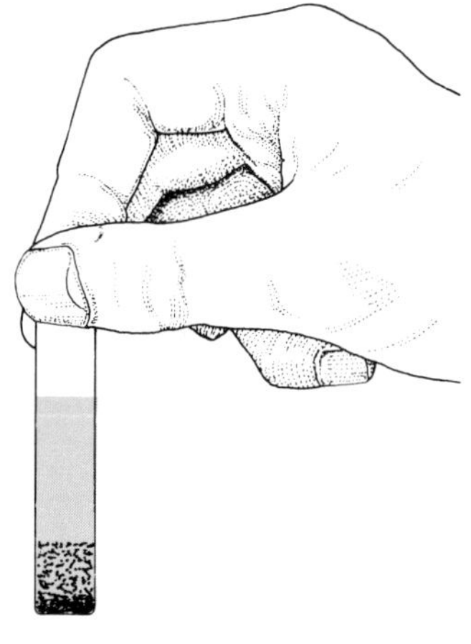

Below **Use a soil-testing kit to find the acidity or alkalinity of the soil. Follow the instructions and match the resulting fluid against the colour chart. A scale known as pH is used to express the degree of acidity or alkalinity**

Alkaline soil This soil occurs mainly where the underlying structure is of chalk or limestone and is often indicated by hard tap water. Many plants grow well in this type of soil and it is better to plant these than to embark on expensive courses of treatment to enable the acid-loving plants to be grown. If you absolutely must have a camellia or rhododendron then consider growing it in a container or peat bed where you have control over the type of soil mix.

The soil, where gardening begins

Peat gardens In gardens with alkaline soil, peat gardens are becoming a popular feature and they make a good solution to the problem of growing lime-hating plants.

First, put down a sheet of polythene and, unless the site is on a slope, make some drainage holes in it. The polythene prevents the lime from finding its way up. The walls of the bed are made from peat blocks laid like bricks. The peat can be bought in blocks of the right size, about 23 by 8 or 10 cm deep (9 by 3 or 4 in deep), and these should be soaked for several hours before use, otherwise they move and slip around and it is never possible to get them really wet. The walls can be built up to whatever height you wish – three courses of the blocks will give you a reasonable planting depth. Once these are complete fill in with a mixture of soil, peat and sand in equal parts and add a little general fertiliser. Then plant up with your favourite lime-hating plants: azaleas, camellias, ericas and primulas are some you might choose.

Acid soil This type of soil occurs in many town and city gardens, is most common in areas where the rainfall is heavy and where the soil is sandy or peaty in texture. Applications of hydrated lime or ground limestone will help to reduce the acidity since all acid soils are low in lime, and the soil-testing kits give an indication of how much lime to apply. The choice of fertiliser for use on this type of soil is important as certain ones, such as sulphate of ammonia, will increase the acidity. If in any doubt stick to a general garden fertiliser.

Finding out about the soil type

The best way of finding out about the kind of soil is by handling it: picking up a small handful and rolling it between the palms of the hands and between the thumb and forefinger.

If it passes through the fingers easily and has a gritty feel when dry, then it is a light soil with a high percentage of sand.

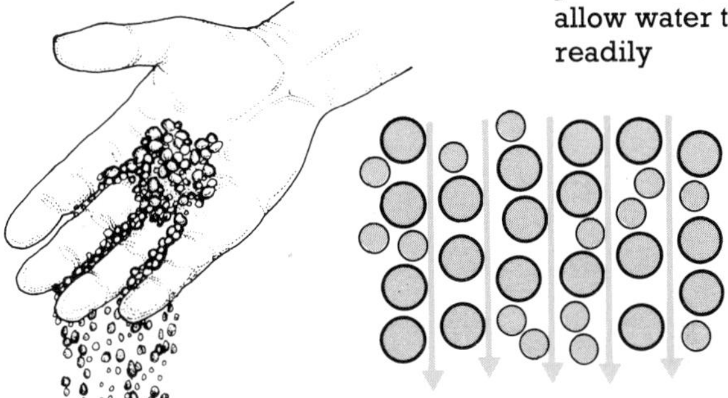

Light soil trickles through the fingers. The large particles and air spaces allow water to drain readily

If it forms small crumbs then it is a medium soil and the ideal one for gardening.

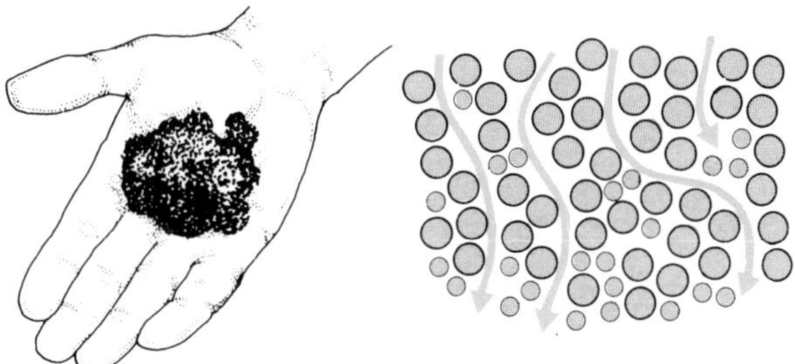

Medium soil, the smaller particles and air spaces mean that water drains more slowly

If it takes a lot of breaking down and smears across the fingers then it is a soil of a heavy or clayey nature. These are heavy soils to work and as well as being slow to dry out they are slow to warm up in the spring. In very dry weather the surface often shows bad cracking.

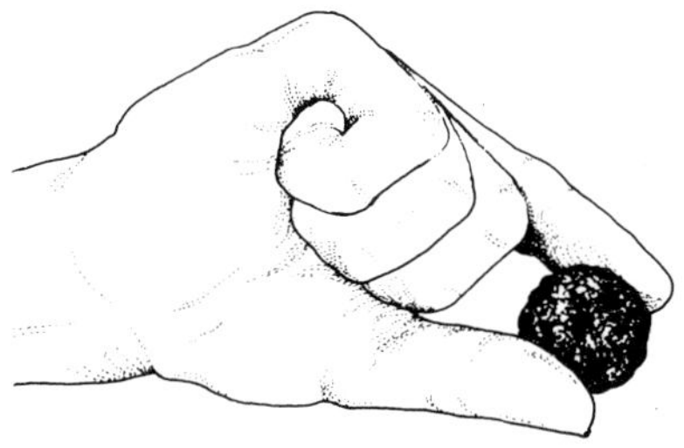

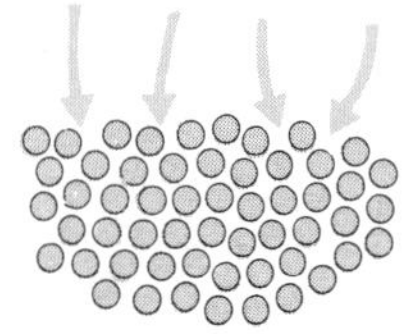

Clay soil forms a solid ball. The small, closely packed particles do not allow the water to drain through easily

The soil, where gardening begins

Plants for alkaline soil

	Height	Planting distance/ spread	Description	Type
Acer campestre (hedge maple)	4·5-6 m (15-20 ft)	3 m (10 ft)	round-headed, good autumn colour	tree
Malus (crab apple)	3-6 m (10-20 ft)	3-6 m (10-20 ft)	blossom in spring, fruits later in the year; rounded head	tree
Berberis (barberry)	1·25-2·5 m (4-8 ft)	1·25-1·5 m (4-5 ft)	orange-yellow flowers in spring followed by red or purple fruits; good autumn colour	shrub
Cornus mas (cornelian cherry)	2·5-3·75 m (8-12 ft)	2-3 m (6-10 ft)	small yellow flowers appear February to April before the leaves; red fruits later in the year	shrub
Euonymus europaeus (spindle tree)	2-3 m (6-10 ft)	1·25-3 m (4-10 ft)	rich autumn colour, poisonous red fruits in autumn	tree
Philadelphus (mock orange)	2-2·75 m (6-9 ft)	2-2·5 m (6-8 ft)	heavily perfumed white flowers	shrub
Aubrieta	8-10 cm (3-4 in)	45-60 cm (1½-2 ft)	flowers in shades of purple in spring	perennial
Clematis	up to 12 m (40 ft)		flowers in shades of yellow, pink, white, purple	climber
Gypsophila	60 cm-1 m (2-3 ft)	30 cm (1 ft)	covered with many small white flowers from June to August	perennial
Narcissus (daffodil)	15-45 cm (6-18 in)	5-15 cm (2-6 in)	yellow or white flowers in spring	bulb
Rudbeckia (Black-eyed Susan)	30 cm-1 m (1-3 ft)	30-60 cm (1-2 ft)	bright yellow flowers with a dark 'eye' in July to October	perennial
Viola (pansy)	5-25 cm (2-10 in)	15-30 cm (6-12 in)	shades of mauve and yellow April to August according to variety	perennial

Improving the soil

Light soil The important points to remember are, first, that this type of soil is not naturally rich in plant foods and so is generally hungry, and, secondly, it does not retain moisture during periods of dry weather. However, it does have the advantage of heating up quickly early in the year and is useful for producing early crops of vegetables.

The key to all soil improvement lies in the addition of organic matter, and in the case of light soils the more organic matter we can get into the soil in the way of peat, garden compost, ground bark or manure, the more we improve the soil. It will help in the retention of moisture and plant foods as well.

Medium soil Although generally considered the most suitable for gardening, this, too, will be improved by digging combined with the incorporation of some form of organic matter.

Vegetables for light soils

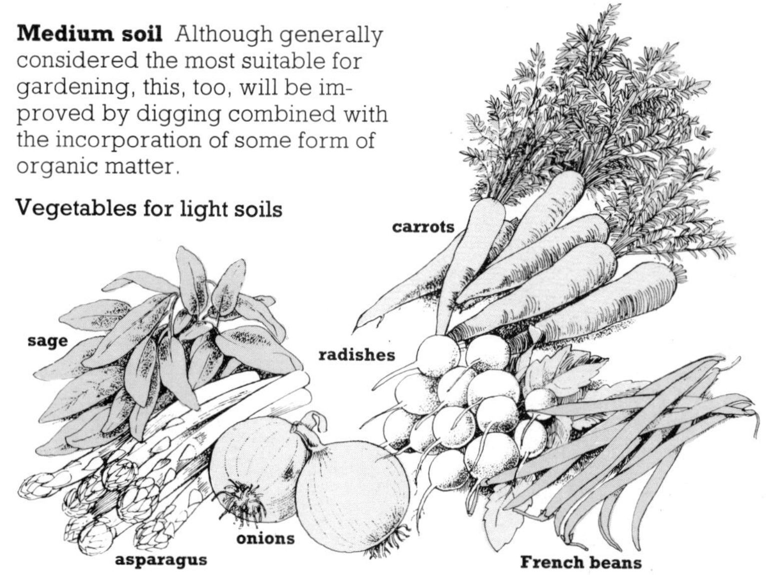

Plants for acid soil

	Height	Planting distance/ spread	Description	Type
Ilex aquifolium (holly)	3-7·5 m (10-25 ft)	2-4·5 m (6-15 ft)	evergreen, berries in winter	tree
Robinia pseudoacacia (false acacia)	6-9 m (20-30 ft)	3-4·5 m (10-15 ft)	cream flowers in June, pale green leaflets	tree
Berberis (barberry)	1·25-2·5 m (4-8 ft)	1·25-1·5 m (4-5 ft)	orange-yellow flowers in spring, red or purple fruits in autumn	shrub
Cistus (rock or sun rose)	1·25-2 m (4-6 ft)	1-2 m (3-6 ft)	pink or white flowers in May to June	shrub
Erica cinerea (bell heather)	23-30 cm (9-12 in)	23-30 cm (9-12 in)	white, pink, maroon flowers in June to October	shrub
Genista hispanica (Spanish gorse)	60 cm-1·25 m (2-4 ft)	2-2·5 m (6-8 ft)	golden yellow flowers in June and July	shrub
Kerria japonica	1·25-2 m (4-6 ft)	1·25-2 m (4-6 ft)	green stems, orange-yellow flowers in April to May	shrub
Juniperus sabina 'Tamariscifolia'	75 cm (2½ ft)	1·5 m (5 ft)	low-growing spreading conifer	conifer
Lonicera periclymenum (honeysuckle)	4·5-6 m (15-20 ft)		sweetly scented, pale yellow flowers July to August	climber
Eryngium maritimum (sea holly)	3·75-5·5 m (12-18 ft)	3·75-5·5 m (12-18 ft)	silver green stem and leaves; metallic blue flowers in July to September	perennial
Kniphofia (red hot poker)	60 cm-1·5 m (2-5 ft)	60 cm (2 ft)	flame, orange, yellow flowers from June to October	perennial
Saxifraga umbrosa (London pride)	30 cm (1 ft)	30-45 cm (1-1½ ft)	pink flowers in May arise from rosette of thick, green leaves	perennial

Vegetables for heavy soils

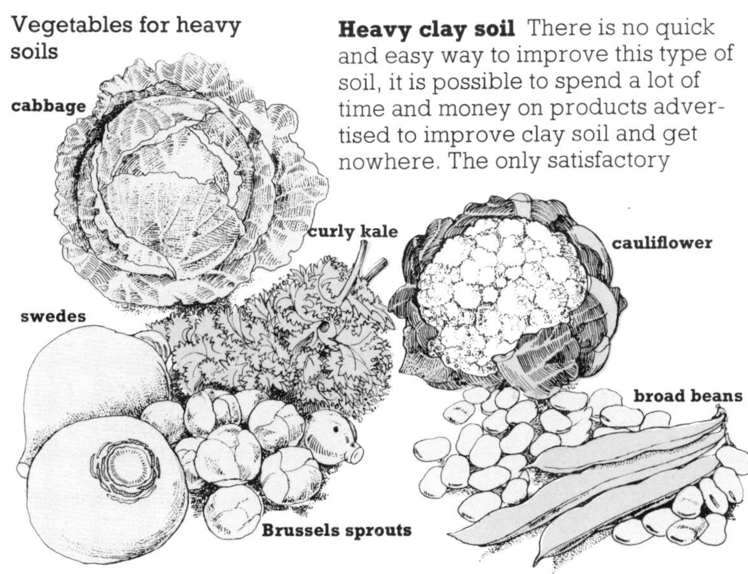

Heavy clay soil There is no quick and easy way to improve this type of soil, it is possible to spend a lot of time and money on products advertised to improve clay soil and get nowhere. The only satisfactory solution is to work in as much organic matter as possible and the soil will gradually become more friable and easier to work.

Good cultivation plays a part in the improvement too, turn the soil over in the autumn leaving the lumps exposed to the weather – frost is one of the finest agents for breaking down clay soils. The addition of ground limestone helps to improve the texture and makes cultivation easier, but this is not a solution where lime-hating plants are to be grown.

One advantage of the heavier soil is that it is generally rather richer in plant food, but as it could be acid or alkaline, soil testing for lime is important.

Digging

There are people who tell us that digging is unnecessary 'Just put on a layer of garden compost and let the worms do the rest'. I would like to think this was right but in fifty years of gardening I have found that the only way of getting good results is by using a spade or a mechanical cultivator.

Soils need to be turned over to the depth of a spade's blade (approximately 25 cm, 10 in – a measurement often known as a spit). Begin by taking out a trench 38 cm (15 in) wide and the depth of a spit to allow room for the soil to be moved forward and turned over as the digging is done. This also allows room for mixing in garden compost, manure or other organic matter. The soil from this trench is moved to the end of the plot as shown in the illustration below.

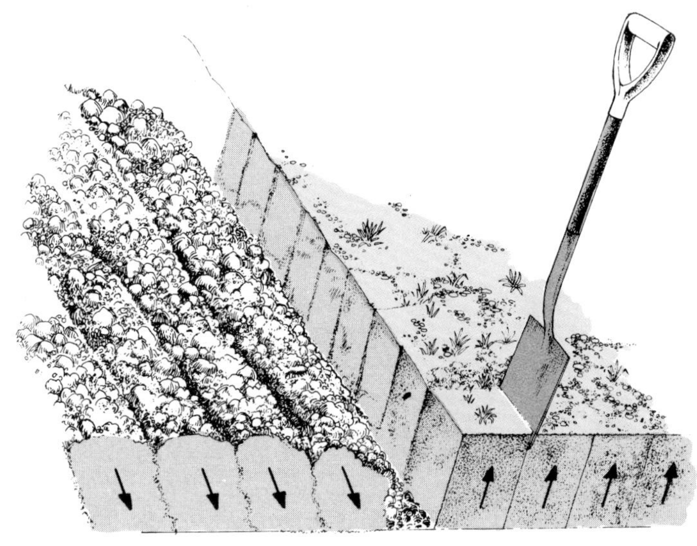

Left **When digging, divide the plot into half and proceed as shown. The soil removed from the first trench is used to infill the last**

Above and below left **Single digging. Each block of soil is moved forward and turned over into the trench. In practice, it may be easier to take over half a block at a time**

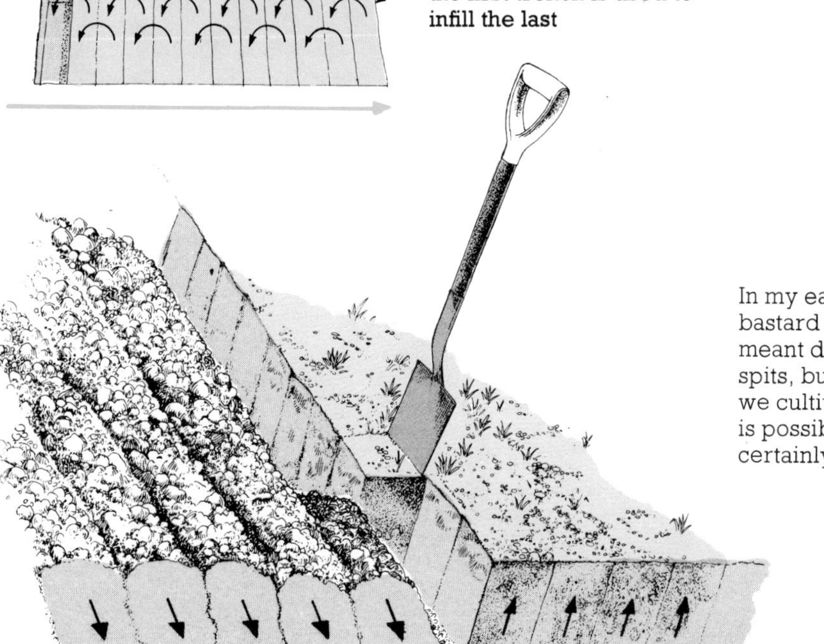

In my early days we always did bastard or double digging which meant digging to a depth of two spits, but customs change and now if we cultivate to the depth of one spit it is possible to grow most things and certainly saves the back muscles.

Important points about digging

1 The soil must be turned over to the depth of one spit.

2 If digging is done in the autumn, so much the better, the soil can then be left in large lumps exposed to the weather. The action of freeze and thaw is helpful in breaking it down. Do not attempt to dig when the soil is wet and sticks to the boots and spade.

3 Dig three weeks to a month before planting to allow time for the natural settling of the soil if digging is not done in the autumn.

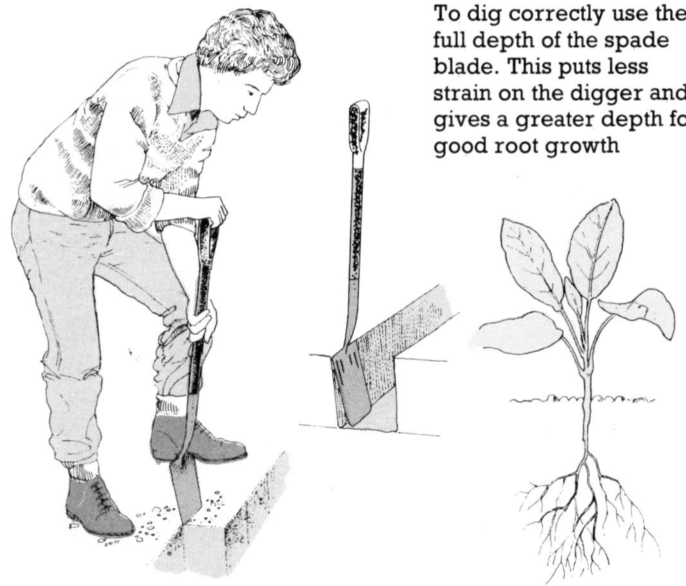

To dig correctly use the full depth of the spade blade. This puts less strain on the digger and gives a greater depth for good root growth

Above **Incorrect digging with the spade at an angle results in shallow cultivation and may stunt root growth**

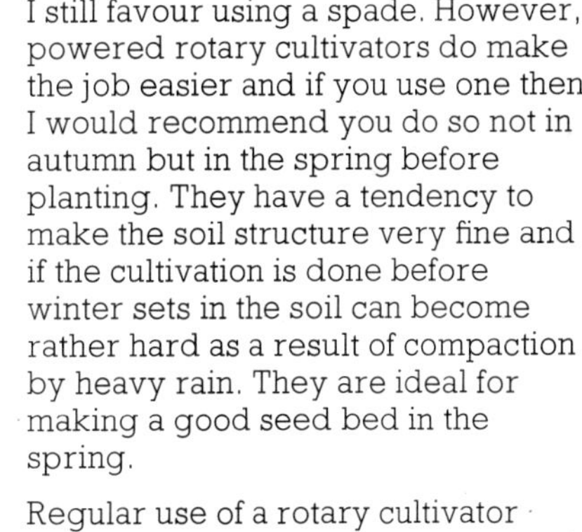

Cultivators

I still favour using a spade. However, powered rotary cultivators do make the job easier and if you use one then I would recommend you do so not in autumn but in the spring before planting. They have a tendency to make the soil structure very fine and if the cultivation is done before winter sets in the soil can become rather hard as a result of compaction by heavy rain. They are ideal for making a good seed bed in the spring.

Regular use of a rotary cultivator tends to bring about the formation of a pan – a layer of compacted soil which prevents roots from penetrating downwards. The occasional digging with a spade will help to break this up.

Below **A rotary cultivator is the easiest way to turn over large areas of ground**

The soil, where gardening begins

Helpful hint

When tackling a new garden it is much easier to get in a contractor to do the initial breaking up for you.

Preparing the new plot

1 The first essential is to clear away any bricks or stones. These can be put on one side to form foundation rubble for paths and paved areas.

2 Dig out any perennial weeds such as couch grass and ground elder – if these are turned over into the soil, the roots break up and a new plant grows from each broken piece.

3 A potato crop can be used as a cleaning crop for weedy soil as the large leafy tops keep down the weeds. They will also help to break up the soil and improve the texture.

Helpful hint

When faced with a new, completely bare garden, I always recommend lightly cultivating the soil, then putting on a dressing of general fertiliser and some peat, ground bark or other organic matter. Rake the surface and sow the whole area with grass seed. The resulting grass can be kept neat and tidy, it is a more relaxing sight than bare soil, gives the children somewhere to play, and allows time to plan the garden. You will have time to think and decide where you want a bed of flowers, a specimen tree, a hedge for privacy, and a vegetable garden. Any unwanted areas of grass can eventually be dug in – this is good for the soil, improves the texture and there is really very little waste.

Plan the garden and in this way make it at your leisure.

The importance of garden compost

Nothing improves soil more than the addition of organic matter, and the cheapest and most easily obtainable form of organic matter is garden compost. In making my compost heap I use all waste from the garden, with the exception of diseased plants and the roots of perennial weeds. After all, anything which comes from the soil can go back into the soil. We add all the kitchen waste, even tea bags, and newspapers can be used if they are shredded and damped down, but then more nitrogen must be added in the form of one of the high nitrogen fertilisers such as Nitrochalk.

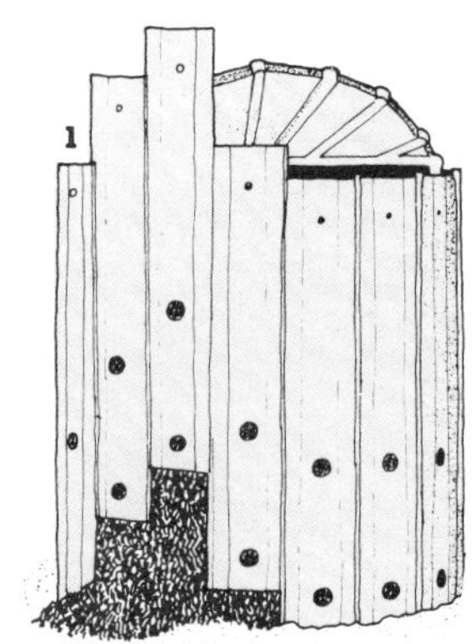

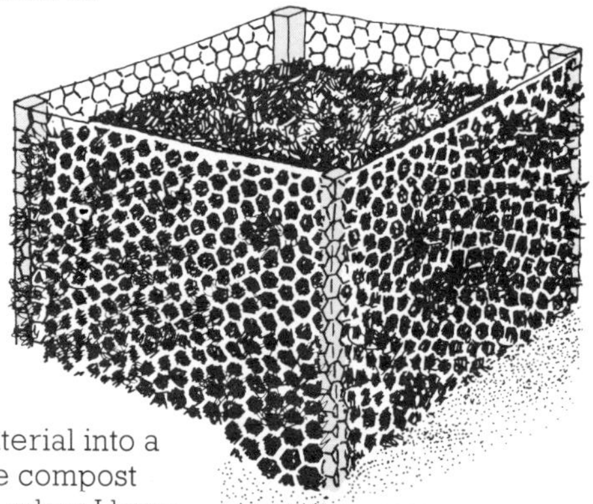

I always put all waste material into a neat pile and not onto the compost heap straightaway. Then, when I have collected a reasonable amount, I put the material onto the heap in 23-cm (9-in) layers, shaking a sprinkling of accelerator over each layer and a light covering of soil. If you can mix in any poultry or other manure this will give a much richer compost.

The bacteria which bring about the decomposition need oxygen to survive, so it is important to build the heap in such a way that air can circulate underneath and round the sides. For the same reason the heap should not be made too big, 1 m (3 ft) high and wide is about right.

It is always advisable to have two heaps on the go, making the compost in one whilst the other is decomposing. It takes an enormous amount of waste material to make a reasonable amount of compost.

Compost bins (1) Sliding panel bin. (2) Wire netting – a side can be unhinged to give access to the compost. (3) Plastic bag

Plants for damp sites

	Height	Spread	Description
Amelanchier canadensis (snowy mespilus)	3 m (10 ft)	3 m (10 ft)	good autumn colour, white star-like flowers in spring
Betula pendula (silver birch)	6-9 m (20-30 ft)	2·5-3·5 m (8-12 ft)	weeping habit, silver bark
Crataegus oxyacantha (hawthorn)	4·5-6 m (15-20 ft)	4·5-5·5 m (15-18 ft)	white flowers in May
Pyrus communis (pear)	4·5-6 m (15-20 ft)	4·5 m (15 ft)	flowers in spring, fruit later in the year
Astilbe x. arendsii	60 cm-1 m (2-3 ft)	30-45 cm (12-18 in)	many varieties available in red, pink, white in June-August; most tolerate moist conditions
Ferns			most tolerate moist conditions
Filipendula ulmaria (meadowsweet)	60 cm-1 m (2-3 ft)	45 cm (18 in)	cream, white, pink flowers in June-July
Iris kaempferi	60-90 cm (2-3 ft)	30-45 cm (12-18 in)	blue, pink, lavender, white in colour in June, July, attractive green-ribbed foliage
Lysimachia nummularia (creeping Jenny)		23-45 cm (9-18 in)	yellow flowers in June-July
Mimulus luteus (monkey musk)	10-60 cm (4-24 in)	30 cm (12 in)	yellow flowers spotted with maroon
Primula (border primulas) in variety	30 cm-1 m (1-3 ft)	23-30 cm (9-12 in)	red, yellow, pink, purple
Rodgersia	1-1·25 m (3-4 ft)	75 cm (2½ ft)	large, attractive leaves, white to deep pink flowers in July
Trollius (globe flower)	60-75 cm (2-2½ ft)	30 cm (1 ft)	yellow flowers in May-June

Rate of decomposition Garden and kitchen waste break down more rapidly in warm, moist conditions. Decomposition is faster in spring and early autumn and in summer provided there is enough moisture in the heap. The average time taken is from four to six months.

Helpful hint

For a small garden or the town garden, small quantities of good compost can be easily and cleanly made in the summer in large black plastic bags, provided these have aeration holes in the sides and drainage holes in the bottom.

Drainage

Comparatively few gardens suffer from bad drainage and these are usually on heavy clay soil. To correct a problem on this scale is a big task and needs to be done properly by experts if it is to be effective. This may well involve the digging of a system of 45- to 60-cm (18- to 24-in) deep trenches in a herringbone pattern with side drains running into a main drain which in turn must slope down to a soakaway.

A general recommendation for improving heavy water-holding soils is to cultivate them in the autumn, digging to the depth of a spade's blade, and leaving the soil in large lumps to be weathered by the frost. Improving the texture by digging in organic matter and giving a dressing of lime also improves drainage.

If the problem is very bad then consider planting moisture-loving plants, building raised beds or growing plants in containers.

Fertilisers and plant feeding

The growth of any plant at any time of the year depends on the temperature, the amount of moisture in the soil, the competition from other plants, and the amount and type of plant foods that are soluble in the soil water. All the time we are expecting more from the soil than the soil alone is capable of giving, and no soil can continue to supply the essential nutrients year after year – the role of the fertiliser is to replace those taken up by the plant.

It is a surprising thought that a green plant is an efficient food factory capable of using water, sunlight, carbon dioxide and various chemical elements to manufacture the food it needs for growth and seed production. The three most important chemicals are nitrogen (N), phosphorus (P) and potassium (K), and all of these must be dissolved in the soil water before they can be taken up by the roots. Plants need a little of each of the nutrients, too much of one and nothing of another does harm.

Other chemicals are needed in smaller quantities, the most important being magnesium, iron and manganese. Lack of these is likely to be a problem on alkaline soils. These chemicals are known as trace elements.

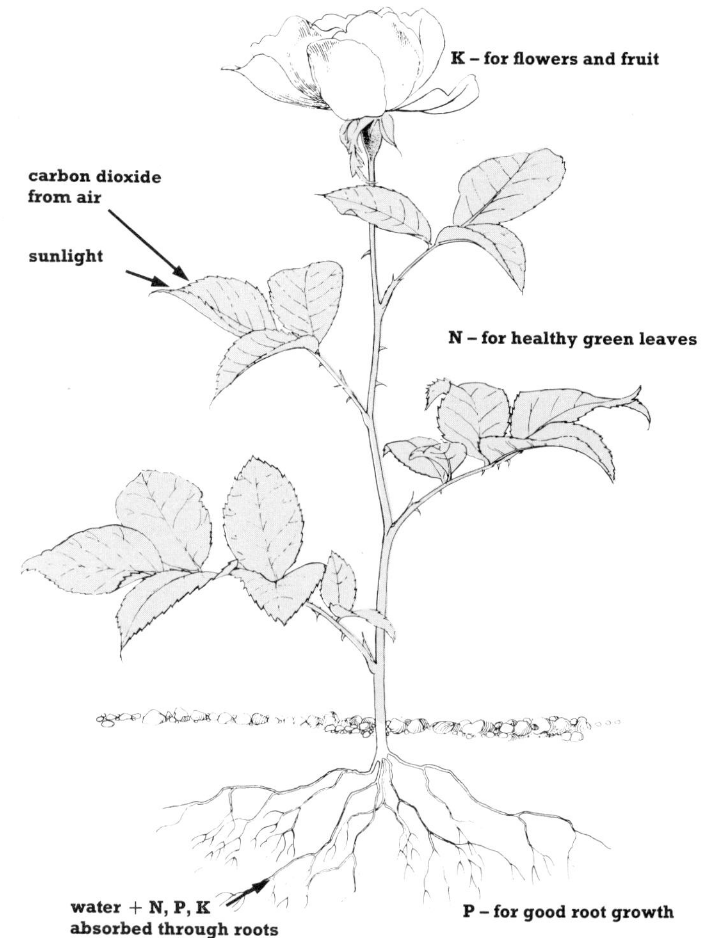

Green plants use carbon dioxide, water, chemicals and sunlight to manufacture their food. The main nutrients – N, P, K – affect different parts of the plant as shown in the illustration. Too much of one nutrient may have a bad effect on the plant and can cause other nutrients to become unavailable to it

Fertilisers and manures

Confusion sometimes occurs between the meaning of these terms; manures are bulky materials of plant or animal origin which in time rot down to form a substance called humus which is responsible for giving soils a friable texture and making them light and easy to work. Manures (or bulky organic fertilisers) have been mentioned earlier as being the ideal way to improve all soils, making clay soils drain more easily while also improving the moisture-holding capacity of light, sandy soils. These are dug in before sowing or planting and they are also put around plants as a mulch.

Fertilisers are non-bulky materials which contain most of the plant nutrients. They are either inorganic – chemicals which are mined from the ground or derived from chemical processes, or they are organic and have a plant or animal origin.

Inorganic fertilisers Of all the inorganic kinds available, my own view is that it is far better to buy a general garden fertiliser which contains a balanced amount of the three essential nutrients, than the individual fertilisers such as superphosphate of lime, and sulphate of ammonia, which supply only one major element and which need care and knowledge in application if they are not to cause an imbalance of plant foods in the soil. Use this for preference in spring before sowing and planting, round growing plants in the early part of the year and then sometimes during the summer months in the case of roses, some shrubs and the vegetables and fruit.

A general fertiliser is also all right for use on lawns unless these are weedy, when it is more usual to choose a lawn fertiliser with added selective weedkiller which takes care of two jobs (weeding and feeding) in one application.

Helpful hint

Save money and keep the brands of fertiliser down. Choose one general garden fertiliser and buy a large quantity – small packets are costly. Roses are an exception, they need extra potash and added magnesium and require a special rose fertiliser. I use the rose fertiliser on all my fruit bushes and trees.

Organic fertilisers These differ from inorganic fertilisers in being much slower to break down in the soil and therefore they release the plant nutrients over a longer period. They are also more expensive. Typical examples are bonemeal, hoof and horn, dried blood, fishmeal and cotton seed meal.

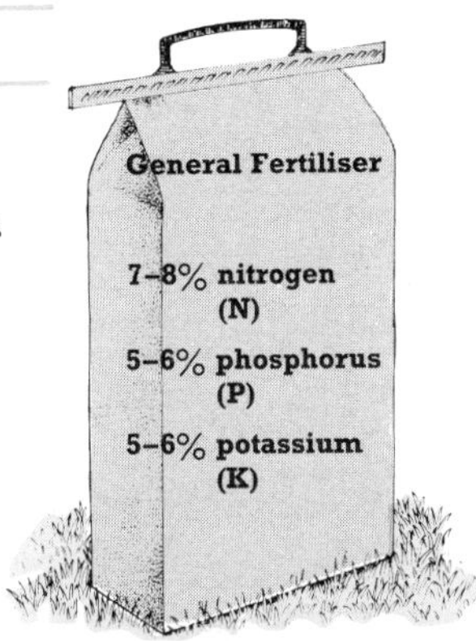

The breakdown of the nutrient content is always shown on the bag. Phosphorus is usually expressed as phosphoric acid, P_2O_5, and potassium as potash, K_2O

N=Nitrogen P=Phosphorus K=Potassium

Organic fertilisers properties and uses

Organic fertiliser	%N	%P	%K	Rate of application	Comments
Dried blood	7-15			30-60 g per sq m (1-2 oz per sq yd)	Nitrogen is available to plants as soon as it is applied. Used as a topdressing for actively growing plants. Often used as a liquid feed as it is fairly soluble.
Bonemeal	3-5	20-30		60-120 g per sq m (2-4 oz per sq yd)	Slow acting, dig in when planting. Phosphorus is available for up to two years and is good for herbaceous borders. The coarser the meal the slower acting it is. Bonemeal increases the alkalinity of the soil.
Hoof and horn	7-15	1-10		60-120 g per sq m (2-4 oz per sq yd)	In the fine grade the nitrogen is available to plants soon after it is applied. Can also be dug in prior to sowing or planting. The coarse grade is good for perennials as it is not easily washed away.
Fishmeal	5-15	6-14		60-120 g per sq m (2-4 oz per sq yd)	Slow acting, also contains valuable trace elements. Dig in about a week before planting. Can be used as a topdressing.
Cottonseed meal	6-9			120-240 g per sq m (4-8 oz per sq yd)	Increases acidity. Dig in before planting or sowing in spring or summer.
Wood ash			4-15	120-240 g per sq m (4-8 oz per sq yd)	Tends to increase alkalinity. Best if dug in in the autumn or winter before sowing or planting. Ash from herbaceous plants and young wood is highest in potassium.
For comparison Fresh farmyard manure	0·6	0·2	0·3	4·5-7·75 kg per sq m (10-15 lb per sq yd)	If composted the nutrient content is increased. Primarily used to improve the structure of the soil.

Fertilisers and plant feeding

Tips for applying fertilisers

1 It is essential to use them carefully or you can waste a lot of time and money. Feed plants from early spring onwards when the roots are growing, not during the winter.

2 Apply at the rate recommended. Little and often is the golden rule.

3 Never put them on near the stems, roots or on the leaves (except for foliar feeds) or they will cause scorching.

4 When applied on a lawn distribute the fertiliser evenly otherwise it will disfigure the grass and may even kill it.

5 Never apply any fertiliser when the soil around the roots is dry, water first even if you are using a liquid fertiliser.

Time of application

General fertiliser is always used as a topdressing and never dug in. If it is dug in a lot of the valuable plant food is lost in drainage. Apply as a dressing before sowing or planting and give an occasional dressing when plants are growing. When used as a topdressing it must be kept away from the stem, sprinkled over the surface and lightly stirred in.

Organic fertilisers, however, are added at the time of digging by being sprinkled along the trench.

Liquid fertiliser

Plants cannot make use of any dry material, all fertilisers have to be broken down first into a soluble form which can then be taken up into the plant dissolved in water from the

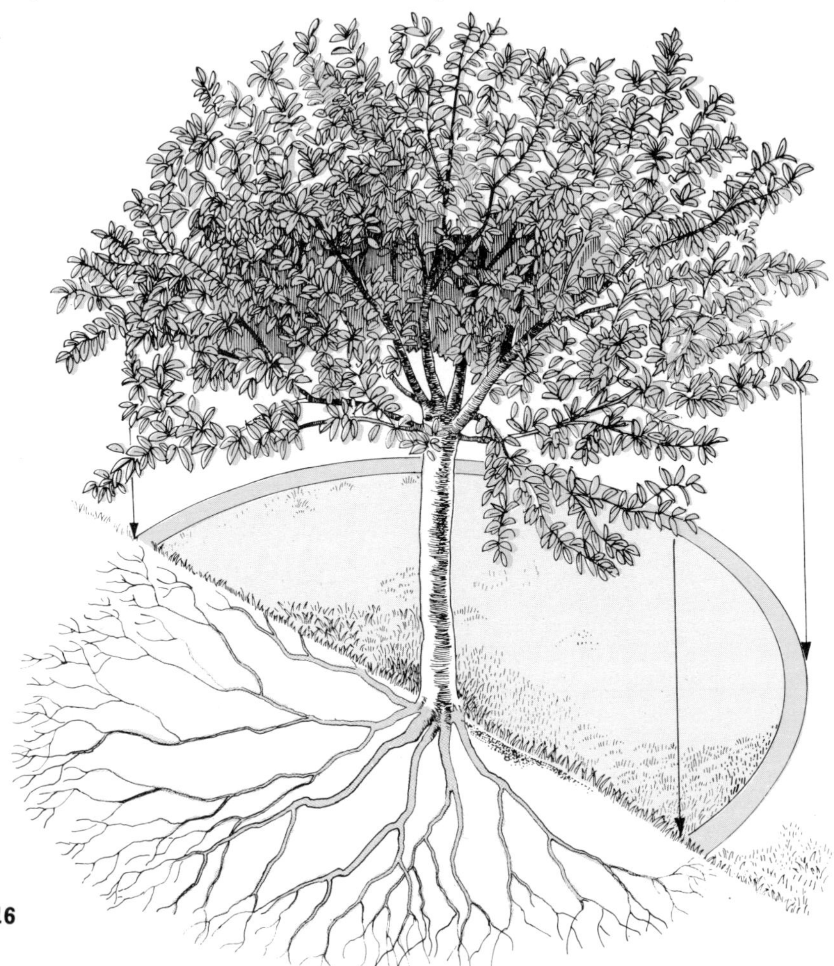

As a rough guide a plant's roots extend as far as the spread of the upper growth. The perimeter of this area is the best position for applying fertiliser as the greatest concentration of fine feeding roots is found here

soil. For this reason liquid fertilisers are generally quicker in action than fertilisers applied in a powdered or granular form but they are not retained by the soil and will be quickly washed through. It is a very convenient way of feeding pot plants and is better for use in the garden in dry weather than granular fertilisers. But they are more expensive and you should assess their value before paying the extra. Provided the moisture is in the soil, I prefer to use the granular or powdered fertilisers which break down more slowly and release their nutrients over a longer period.

At one time we used a cheap and effective liquid fertiliser made from natural animal manures. This was mixed with a pot of soot and put into a bag which was then dropped into a tank of water and left for three days. The resulting liquid was further diluted to a light straw colour (approximately 1 part to 3 parts of water) before use.

Foliar feeds As well as absorbing food through their roots, plants can take in food through their leaves and there are special fertilisers available for this purpose. One point to remember is that they should not be used in dry weather unless there is some moisture at the plant's roots.

Feeding routine

All garden plants benefit from a dressing of general fertiliser in the spring as they are starting into growth. But for some plants regular feeding is especially important: roses grow rapidly and should be fed early in spring and then three or four times during the summer and for these I use a rose fertiliser which contains extra potash and magnesium as well as the basic nutrients.

Fruit trees should be fed in spring and for these I also use a rose fertiliser.

Vegetables need a basic dressing of fertiliser immediately before seed sowing and an occasional top-dressing as they are growing.

All house plant potting composts contain fertiliser but this eventually has to be supplemented because plants grown in a very restricted root space quickly exhaust the supply and need extra food. Use either a liquid fertiliser or a tiny pinch of general fertiliser.

Lime and liming

Lime is the term used to describe the inorganic chemicals such as hydrated lime which result by one process or another from chalk or limestone rocks. Soils overlying limestone rocks tend to contain a quantity of weathered chalk and are usually alkaline in reaction. Apart from its effect on the soil in this way, lime is a useful material for increasing the fertility of the soil and also for improving the texture of heavy clay soil by causing the tiny particles to clump together in small crumbs.

Applying lime

1 An average dressing of hydrated lime would be 75 g to the sq m (3 oz to the sq yd). Ground limestone is used at twice the rate.

2 Apply between October and February.

3 Never apply at the same time as manure or other fertiliser because it either reacts chemically with them or makes them less soluble.

4 Sprinkle over the surface and leave it to be washed in by the rain.

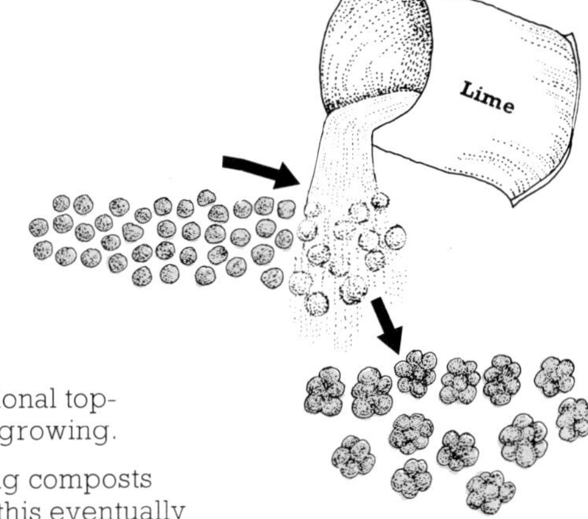

When applied to a heavy soil, lime causes the tiny particles to clump together, thus increasing the size of the air spaces and improving the soil texture

The importance of mulching

A mulch is, quite simply, a covering for the soil which has the effect of increasing its moisture retention and keeping down weeds. The advantages are more clearly seen on a light soil than on a medium or heavy one but, used properly, mulches are of great benefit to all garden plants and particularly to vegetable and fruit crops.

If the soil is left uncovered in summer, the sun and wind cause a lot of the soil moisture to evaporate and this brings about a need for more frequent watering. The mulch, acting as an insulating layer, cuts down evaporation with the result that the plant roots can remain in the richest food layer near the surface instead of having to delve deeper after water.

In order to be effective as a weed-control measure, the mulch must be at least 5 cm (2 in) thick.

A black plastic mulch can be used for growing potatoes

Mulching a shrub. The mulch extends as far as the edge of the leaf canopy; it is important that it does not touch the stem

Materials for mulching

All the substances used to add organic matter to the soil make equally good mulching materials. The principal among these are decayed manure, garden compost, peat, ground bark, spent mushroom compost, spent hops. Sheets of plastic are also effective and black plastic is helpful in keeping down weed growth.

Using mulches

The mulching material is spread on the ground around the plant leaving an area immediately around the stem free. It is important not to put the mulch on too early in the year before the soil has had a chance to warm up as the organic materials used tend to reflect the heat and reduce the level of solar radiation reaching the soil – if the soil is cold when the mulch goes on it will remain cold.

Plastic, on the other hand, absorbs the heat and allows the sun's rays through and the soil beneath warms up quickly. But this should not be put on while there is a danger of frost as the plastic in warming the soil causes a layer of moisture to collect on the underside and this has a tendency to draw the frost.

Plastic mulches are lifted at the end of the summer and carefully stored for further use. Organic mulches will mostly decompose and be washed into the soil. Any material left can be dug in provided the area of the feeding roots is avoided.

Mulching with stones is effective and attractive

Special uses of mulches

1 Plastic, used as a mulch around newly planted trees and shrubs, does much to help them get established by preventing loss of moisture from the soil.

2 Black plastic provides a novel way of growing potatoes: lay strips of the plastic 45 to 60 cm (18 to 24 in) wide on well cultivated ground and place the seed potatoes on the surface below the plastic at intervals of 38 cm (15 in). Make a cross cut over each potato to allow the leaves and stems to grow through. The great advantage of this is that the plastic can be lifted at intervals as the potatoes form and the large ones picked off while the others are left to develop further.

It is essential not to plant under the plastic too early in the year or the frost will penetrate and kill the roots and tops.

3 When placed around strawberry plants instead of straw, plastic helps to conserve the soil moisture as well as keeping the fruit clean.

4 Spread a layer of plastic on the ground before standing out any pots of plants. The plastic prevents the plants rooting down into the soil, and stops weeds from growing between them.

5 A layer of large pebbles over the roots of trees and shrubs acts as a mulch and makes a most effective garden feature.

Water and watering

Correct watering is the most difficult task that the gardener has to learn. Most garden plants draw their moisture from the soil near the surface, this in turn is constantly losing water through the plants and by evaporation. But to give too much water is as bad as giving too little. Good root growth requires a soil which allows air to pass freely through the pore spaces; waterlog the soil, fill the pore spaces, and you stop the root growth and eventually kill the plant. Too little water has an equally bad effect, in that plants are subjected to too much stress if they have difficulty in drawing up the water they need because there is insufficient in the soil and what moisture that is present is held tightly in the soil structure.

Watering depends on soil type

Each type of soil has a different capacity for holding water. Clay, for example, can hold much more than sand, although the water-holding capacity of the latter can be improved by digging in organic matter. Whatever the soil type, until the water-holding capacity of each layer of soil is exceeded, the water will not move deeper into the soil. This is the reason why one often finds that although the top few inches are wet the soil underneath is dry. In gardens where there is a strong prevailing wind, water loss from the soil can be cut down by planting a windbreak.

Right The rotating water sprinkler sprays water in a circular pattern (*far right*)

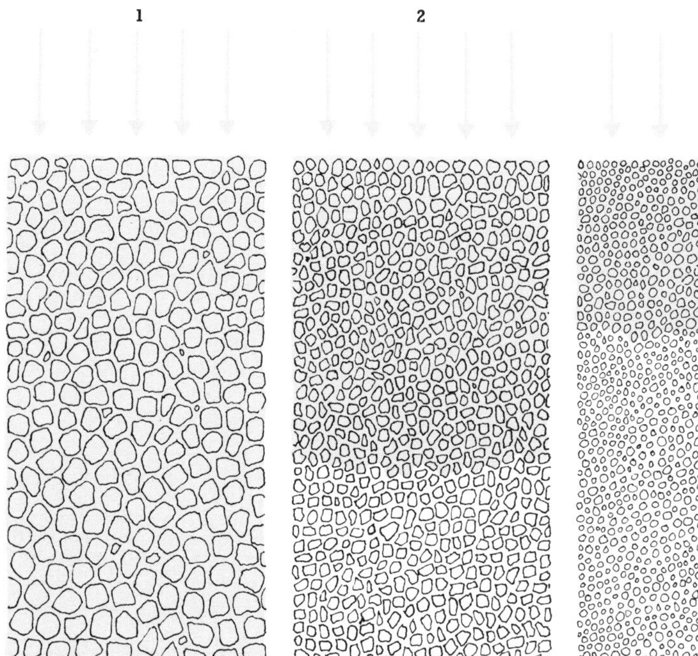

Left Diagram to illustrate the water-holding capacity of different types of soil. The coloured areas show the approximate depth to which 2·5 cm (1 in) of water will penetrate. (1) Sandy soil (2) Medium soil (3) Clay soil

Right The oscillating water sprinkler has a rectangular spray pattern (*far right*)

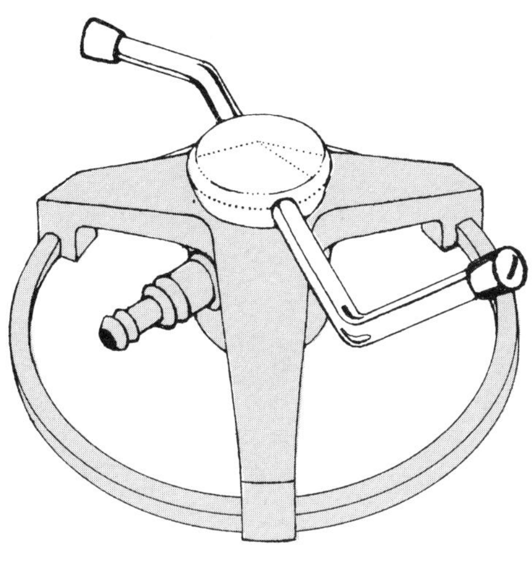

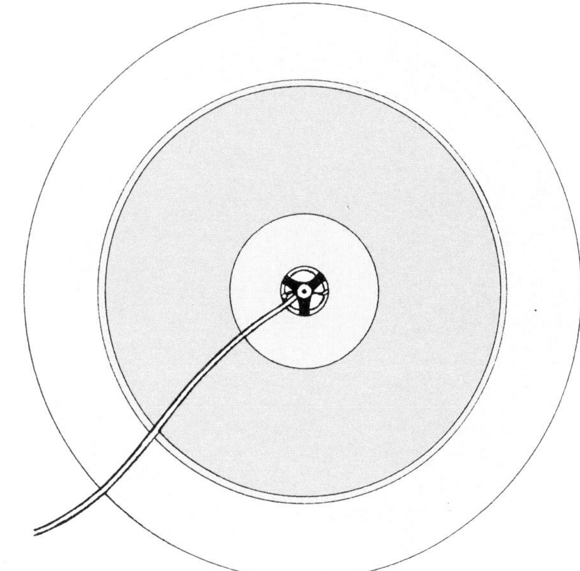

Key to the diagrams of spray patterns

Least water falls in this area

Some water falls in this area

Most water falls in this area

How to water Watering in the correct way is all important, a heavy deluge is no good as this simply causes compaction of the surface and much of the water runs off without soaking in. Equally bad are frequent light waterings which wet only the upper few inches and encourage shallow rooting as well as leading to a lot of water evaporation. Ideally, the soil should be gently and thoroughly soaked and then not watered again until the surface starts to dry out.

Equipment

The easiest way to water correctly is by using a sprinkler attachment for the hose. There are two main kinds – the oscillating and the rotary. Do not use sprinklers in windy weather as the water droplets get carried away before they can penetrate the soil.

Drip irrigation equipment of various types is available and this cuts down the time involved in watering. One big disadvantage, however, is that it waters every plant whether it is needed or not.

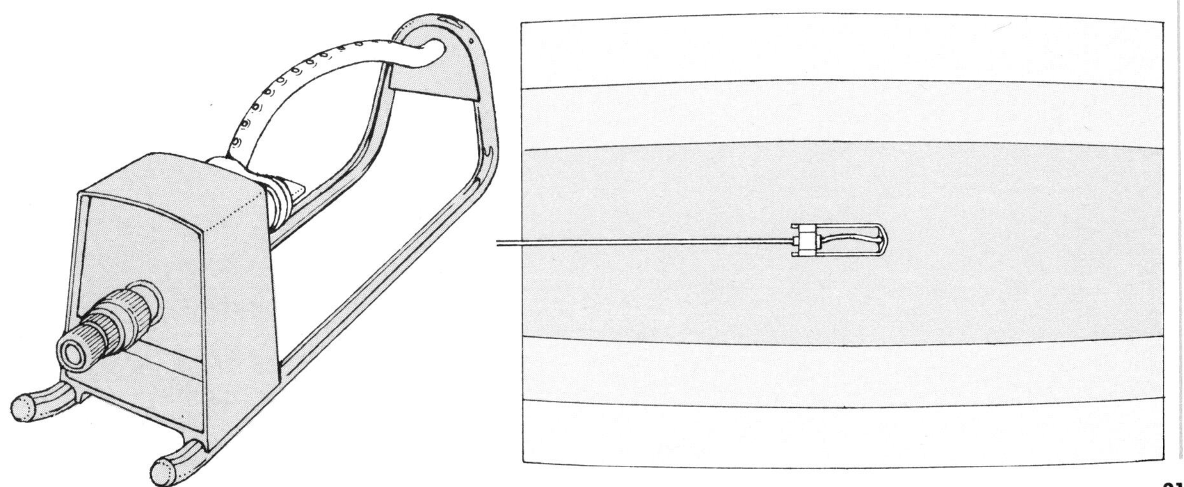

Water and watering

Hose Some hosepipes have tiny holes all along their length and this allows quite large areas to be watered at the same time.

When watering with a hose, make sure you break the force of the spray with either an adjustable nozzle or by placing a thumb over the end. A hose with a nozzle attachment can be propped in place by supporting it through the handle of a spade or fork but the water is then directed only one way, and the spade must be continually moved. It is better to invest in a sprinkler.

When buying a hose, make sure you get one long enough, or join two together with a hose connector. A reel is useful both for storing the hose in good condition and making it easier to use.

Hoses are available in different diameters: $\frac{5}{8}$in is a practical size for most gardens but if there are a lot of trees and shrubs then a large one, $\frac{3}{4}$in, would be a better buy. The larger the diameter, the more water the hose can deliver. However, hoses with diameters exceeding $\frac{3}{4}$in are difficult and heavy to handle.

Watering cans A large watering can is an essential piece of equipment for any size of garden and is especially useful for watering individual plants and those grown in containers and pots. For watering seedlings and cuttings the force of water emerging from the spout needs to be broken up into a spray pattern by an attachment called a rose, otherwise the water will flatten the plants.

Watering transplanted trees and shrubs

One of the main reasons for the failure of newly planted trees and shrubs is that because of the disturbance to the roots, the leaves and stems lose moisture faster than the roots can take it up. And this can be a problem particularly with conifers (see page 43). All newly planted trees and shrubs will benefit from being sprayed overhead to reduce the loss of water from the leaves.

In dry weather it is essential to make the best use of any available water. Planting in a depression (*below left*) keeps the water over the root area. Similarly (*below*), vegetables such as beans can be grown in a trench which can be flooded from time to time

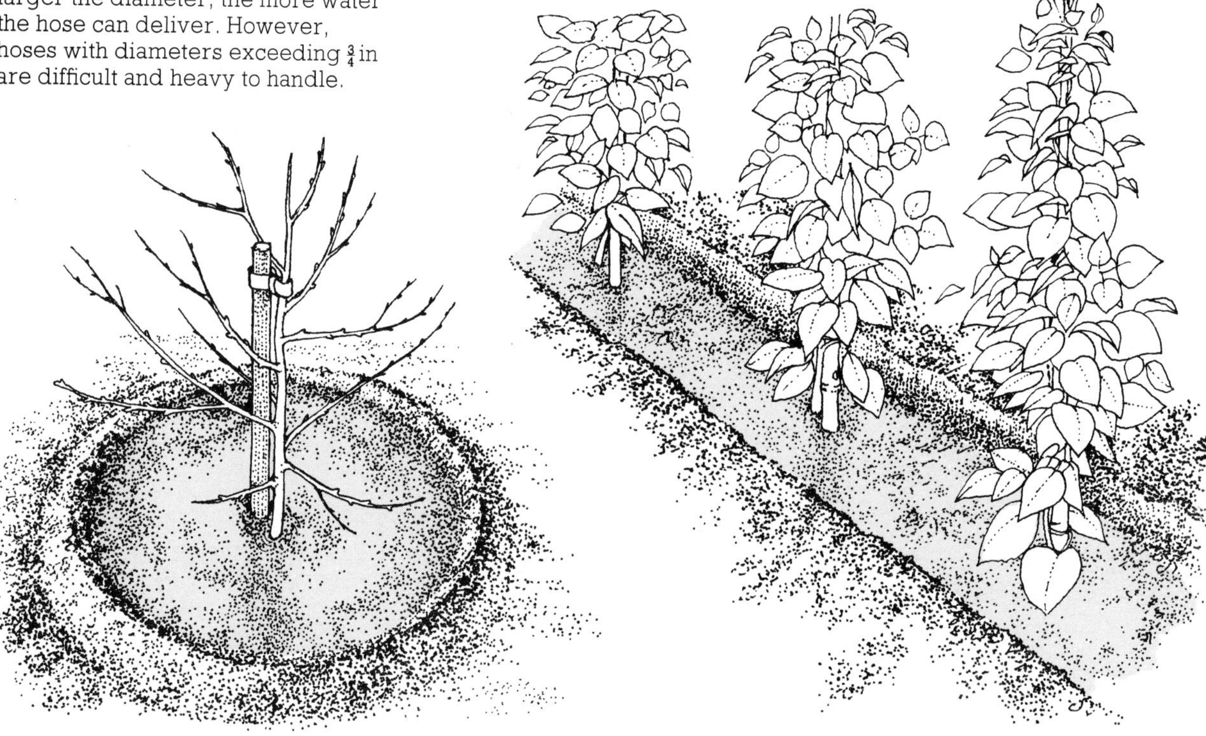

Water and watering

Below Sink a flower pot by a tomato plant at planting time and water through this to enable the water to filter out at root level where it is most needed. *Below left* A hose pipe with holes at intervals directs water to the plants

Helpful hint

Stones placed over the root area of shrubs such as clematis cut down evaporation from the soil, and a layer of peat topped with stones put over the centre of creeping plants such as the heathers causes water to collect and encourages roots to form.

Watering cuttings

Cuttings are easier to root and more likely to be successful if water loss is cut down in some way, such as by covering with plastic, see page 36.

Watering vegetables

Vegetables need a plentiful supply of water if they are to crop satisfactorily. However, if watering restrictions are in force then the order of priority is as follows: runner beans, celery, lettuce, newly planted cabbage and related crops, peas and onions. Making sure that the water gets to where it is required is also important and planting in trenches or depressions in the soil is a useful means of water conservation.

Watering pot plants

Plants growing within the confines of a pot are especially vulnerable to lack of moisture in warm weather because of the limited amount of compost. Check their requirements daily and water well either using a watering can or by submerging the pot in a container of water and leaving it until bubbles cease to rise from the surface of the compost. Grouping plants together or sinking the pot into an outer container of moist peat are measures which will cut down evaporation and water loss from the plants.

Helpful hint

One sure way of finding out if a pot plant requires water is by lifting the pot and feeling the weight. A light pot indicates the need for more moisture.

Make watering as effective as possible

1 Put in a windbreak.

2 Dig in as much organic matter as possible.

3 Mulch with organic matter or plastic.

4 Use a sprinkler.

5 Plant in trenches or depressions.

Lawns and lawn care

Grass is the easiest crop in the world to grow provided it is treated as a plant: cultivate it, feed it, keep it healthy and you will find it will respond better than any other plant in the garden.

Lawns can be made by sowing grass seed or by laying turf and I always think that it is far easier and better to start with seed. Economically, too, it makes sense as the cost of seed will be 25 per cent or less than that of turf. The initial preparation, however, is the same for both methods.

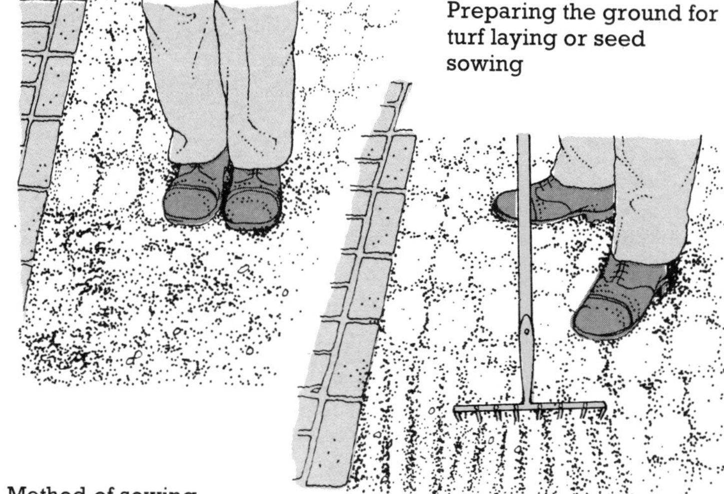

Preparing the ground for turf laying or seed sowing

Preparing the ground

Break up the soil to a depth of 15 to 20 cm (6 to 8 in), using either a spade or fork, and at the same time work in peat, ground bark, garden compost or rotted manure to improve the texture. Do this at least a month before making the lawn to allow time for the soil to settle.

Firm the soil well by treading backwards and forwards over it and rake to achieve a fine even surface.

Apply a dressing of general fertiliser at 55 gm per sq m (2 oz per sq yd) and rake again.

Too much is said about the need to get an absolutely level surface, as long as it is even enough for the mower to go over, some gentle undulations are an advantage to the lawn.

Method of sowing – divide the ground into metre squares to aid even sowing

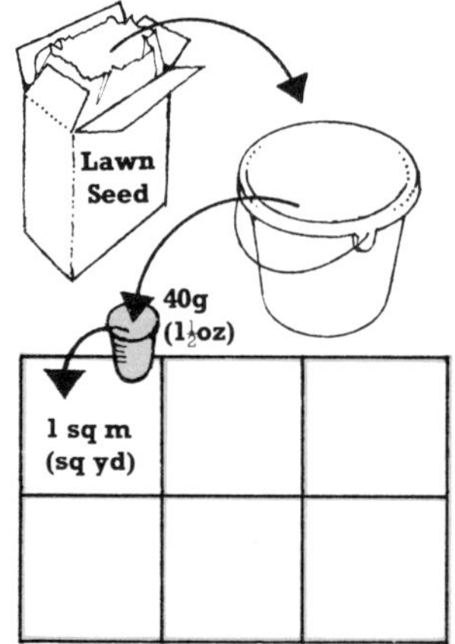

Lawns from seed

It is good policy to buy the best lawn seed mixture – one which does not contain rye grass – even if the finished surface will have to stand up to a lot of wear and tear. The coarse grasses, and the indigenous grasses, will come in later anyway. Another advantage of buying mixtures of the finer grasses is that these are slower in growth and are easier to maintain.

The best time to sow is from late March to early June, or from early September to early October. Avoid dry hot spells. Use seed dressed with bird repellent or cover the seeded area with nets to keep birds away.

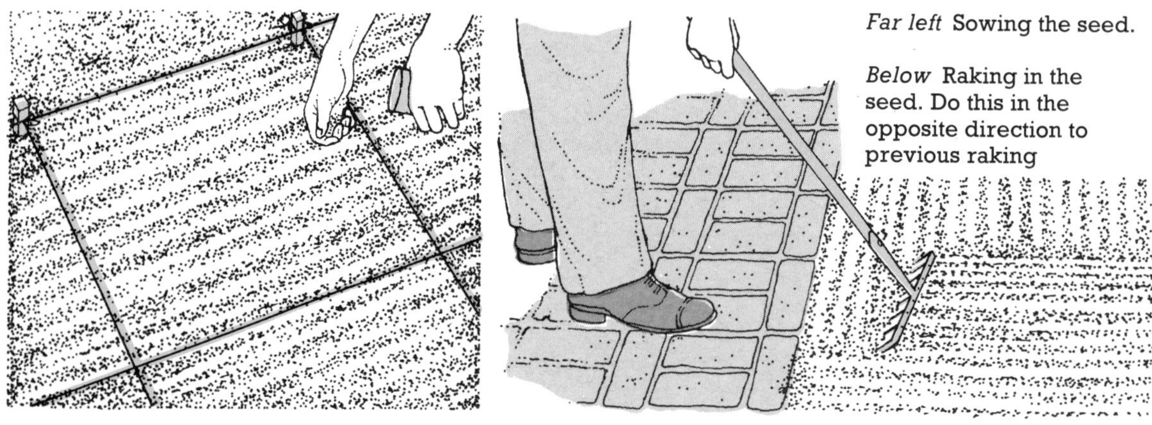

Far left Sowing the seed.

Below Raking in the seed. Do this in the opposite direction to previous raking

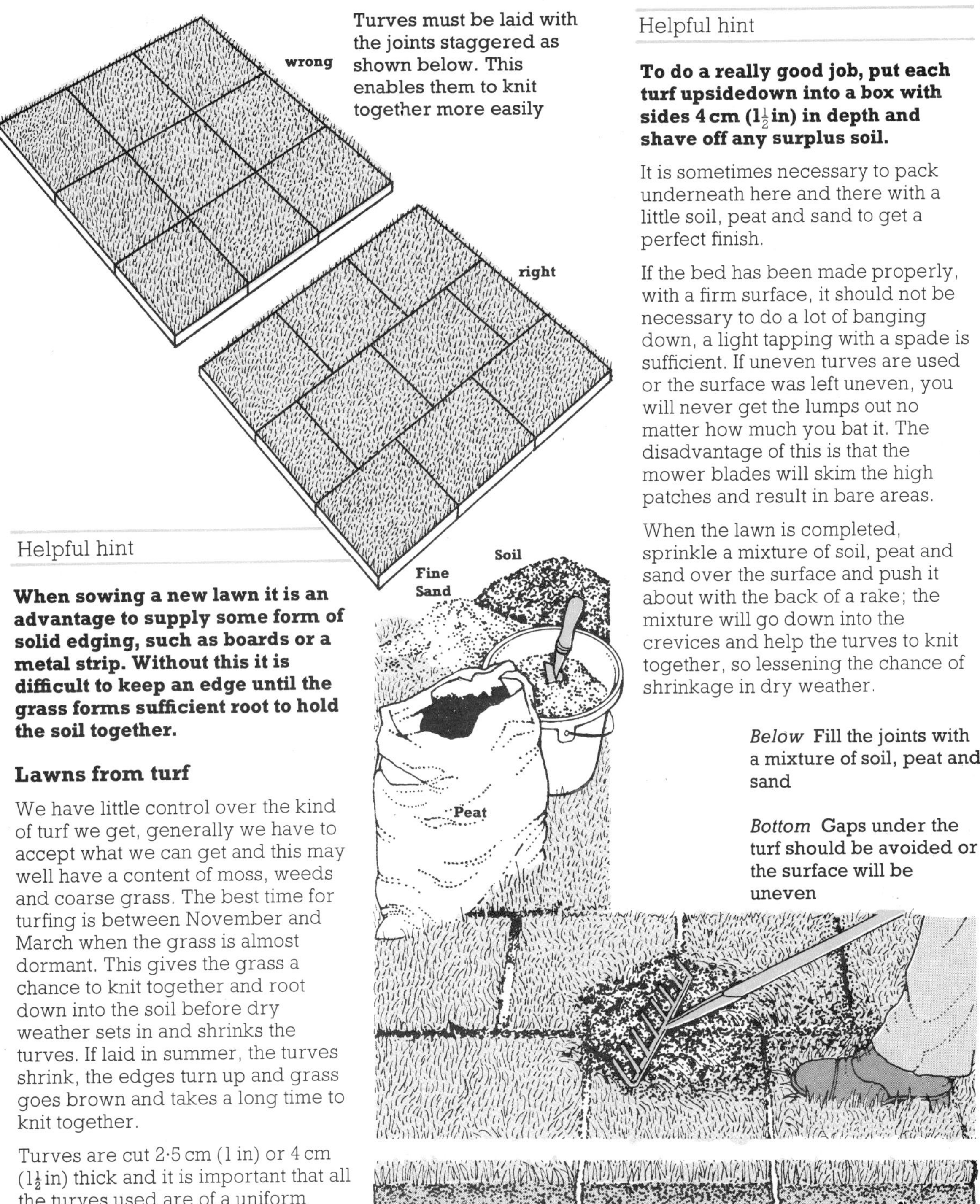

Turves must be laid with the joints staggered as shown below. This enables them to knit together more easily

Helpful hint

When sowing a new lawn it is an advantage to supply some form of solid edging, such as boards or a metal strip. Without this it is difficult to keep an edge until the grass forms sufficient root to hold the soil together.

Lawns from turf

We have little control over the kind of turf we get, generally we have to accept what we can get and this may well have a content of moss, weeds and coarse grass. The best time for turfing is between November and March when the grass is almost dormant. This gives the grass a chance to knit together and root down into the soil before dry weather sets in and shrinks the turves. If laid in summer, the turves shrink, the edges turn up and grass goes brown and takes a long time to knit together.

Turves are cut 2·5 cm (1 in) or 4 cm (1½ in) thick and it is important that all the turves used are of a uniform thickness or you will not get an even surface.

Helpful hint

To do a really good job, put each turf upsidedown into a box with sides 4 cm (1½ in) in depth and shave off any surplus soil.

It is sometimes necessary to pack underneath here and there with a little soil, peat and sand to get a perfect finish.

If the bed has been made properly, with a firm surface, it should not be necessary to do a lot of banging down, a light tapping with a spade is sufficient. If uneven turves are used or the surface was left uneven, you will never get the lumps out no matter how much you bat it. The disadvantage of this is that the mower blades will skim the high patches and result in bare areas.

When the lawn is completed, sprinkle a mixture of soil, peat and sand over the surface and push it about with the back of a rake; the mixture will go down into the crevices and help the turves to knit together, so lessening the chance of shrinkage in dry weather.

Below Fill the joints with a mixture of soil, peat and sand

Bottom Gaps under the turf should be avoided or the surface will be uneven

Lawns and lawn care

Mowers

For very small lawns, a hand-propelled side-wheel or roller-type mower is all that is needed, but the majority of lawns require a powered mower. There is a range of battery, electric and motor mowers to suit all purposes and pockets. It is always better to have a mower slightly larger than you think you need. This makes the job easier and does not work the machine to death.

For a rough area of lawn or orchard, and for cutting round trees and between shrubs, nothing beats a rotary. For banks, choose an air cushion mower, but remember that for the careless these are the finest toe choppers in the world, so take care and wear a solid pair of shoes when using them.

There are two main types of mowers: the cylinder or reel and the rotary.

Cylinder mowers are of two kinds depending on whether they are driven by wheels or rollers. The wheel version is the cheaper and good for cutting rough grass but the roller is better as it can be operated over the lawn edge, gives a smoother finish and leaves the banded effect seen on the best lawns.

Both types are available in a number of widths – 30, 35 or 45 cm (12, 14 or 18 in) are the most common – and as either hand-propelled or powered machines. Another variation lies in the number of cuts the machine makes to the yard run – the higher the number the smoother the cut; most hand machines make between 45 and 60 cuts, but the rather higher rate of the powered machines is to be preferred.

Rotary mowers are especially good for long grass but they do not give the banded effect of the roller cylinder mower. They are always power propelled and are either driven by wheels or float on an air cushion like a hovercraft. The last are particularly good for cutting grass on banks and slopes.

All types of powered mowers are propelled by a petrol engine, or by electricity used either directly from the mains by means of a cable (which must be kept away from the cutting blades) or provided by a battery. The petrol engine is the best for larger areas. The battery is reliable but does make the machine rather heavy; batteries need recharging every two hours.

Maintenance of machines

Any lawn mower which has had a busy season should go away for an overhaul and to have the blades sharpened in the winter. Otherwise you start the year with a mower in poor condition which will in all likelihood let you down in the middle of the busy mowing season.

Check the oil in the sump at regular intervals and always use the recommended petrol or petrol and oil mixture.

When not in use always detach the suppressor cap (with lead) from the sparking plug, otherwise the engine can start if the blades are turned. This is especially important if children are around.

Always store in a cool, dry place.

Adjusting a cylinder mower

Never set the blade too low. For established grass the blade should not be less than 1 cm ($\frac{1}{2}$ in) from the soil surface. To check the height, turn the mower over, and put a straight edge (board) from the front roller to the back roller – the space between the bottom blade and the board indicates the height of the cut. For a newly sown lawn adjust the blade to give a clearance of 4 cm ($1\frac{1}{2}$ in) above soil level for the first cut. Succeeding cuts in the first summer should allow 2·5 cm (1 in) from the soil surface.

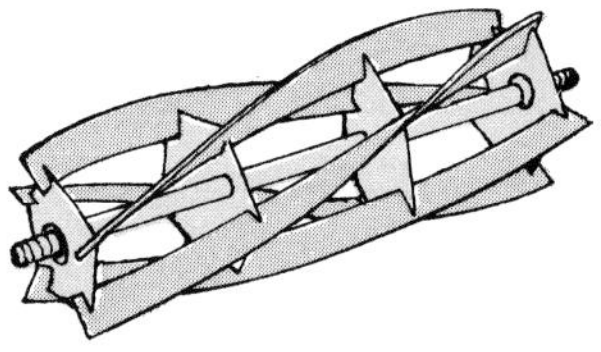

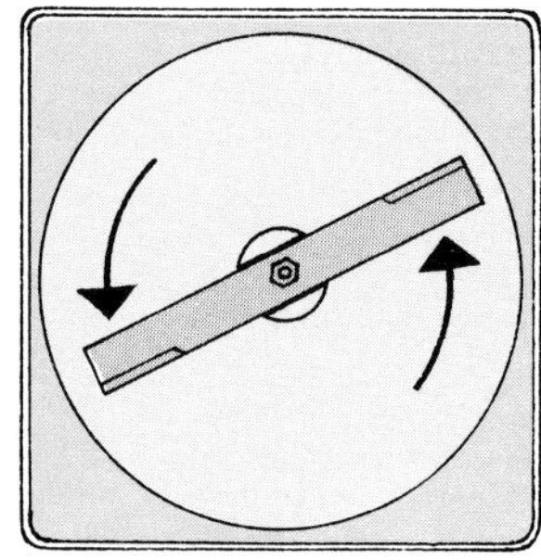

Top Blade from a cylinder mower

Above Cutting blade on the underside of a rotary mower

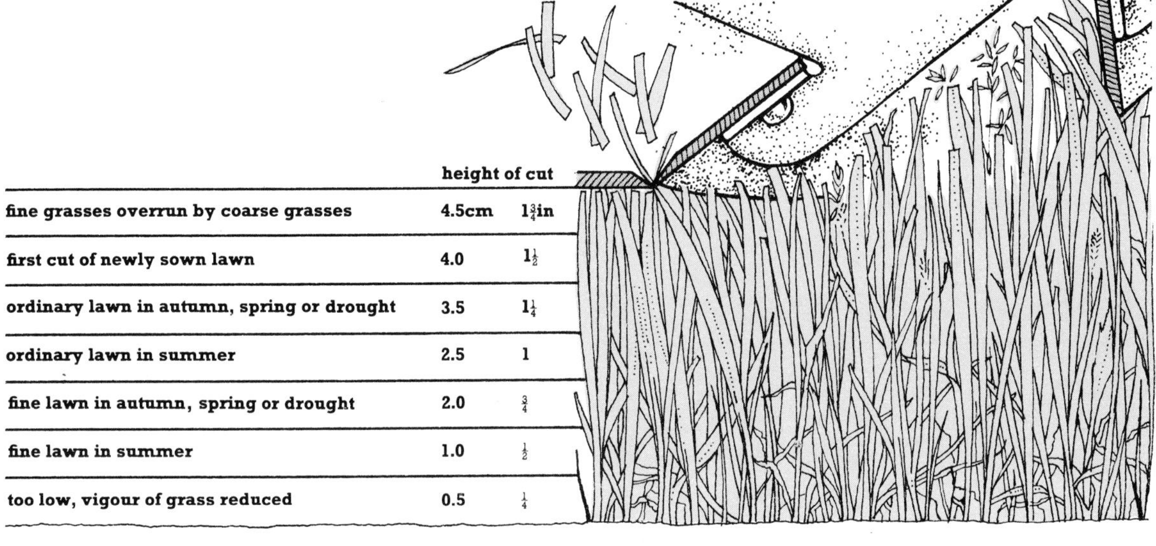

	height of cut	
fine grasses overrun by coarse grasses	4.5cm	1¾in
first cut of newly sown lawn	4.0	1½
ordinary lawn in autumn, spring or drought	3.5	1¼
ordinary lawn in summer	2.5	1
fine lawn in autumn, spring or drought	2.0	¾
fine lawn in summer	1.0	½
too low, vigour of grass reduced	0.5	¼

To achieve a good finish the sharpness of the blade is all important. Test this by placing a piece of paper against the bottom blade and revolving the cylinder by hand, if it cuts the paper cleanly, it will cut the grass cleanly without tearing the young plants up from the soil.

Above The height of the mower blade should be adjusted to give the correct cut for the type of grass or time of the year

Below Method of mowing. Cut first around the edge of the lawn and any beds

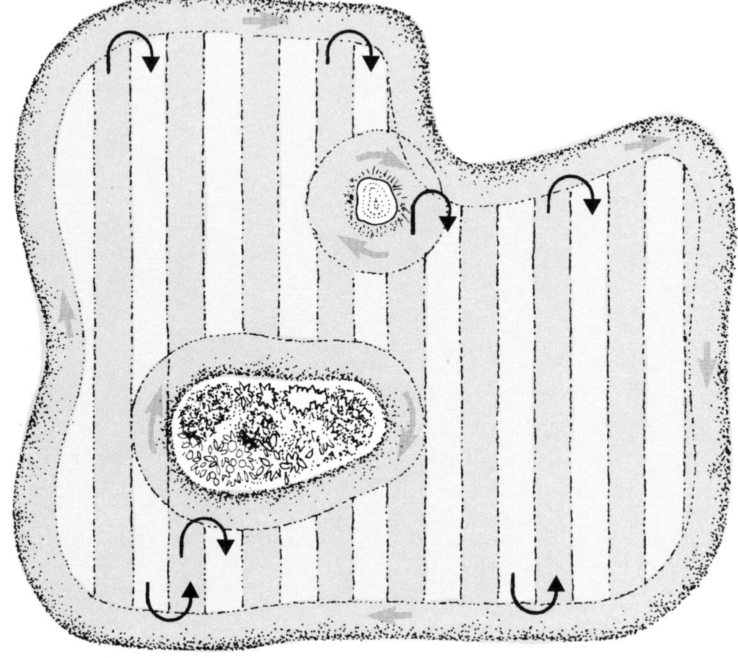

Mowing

I like to go round the outside of the lawn first to give a turning space, then round awkward places around trees and beds. Only after doing this do I cut backwards and forwards. Keep each cut straight to get perfect banding, although this will only be possible with a cylinder mower. If the grass is mown often, the clippings can be left where they fall, otherwise they should be collected up with a springbok rake if the mower is without a collecting box.

The lawn is easier to maintain if it is cut frequently. If the grass is allowed to get too long, the mower chews some of it and leaves lumps, so you will need to go over it a second time. Cut every week or ten days and you will find the lawn is better for it and there is less grass to take away.

The first mowing of the year is usually done in early spring as soon as the grass starts growing and the last in late autumn.

Never mow or go on the lawn more than you can help when it is very wet. Movement on the lawn then will seal the soil surface, affecting the health of the grass and encouraging moss and weeds.

Lawns and lawn care

Helpful hint

In spring or autumn, when there is a heavy dew on the grass, the lawn will dry out faster if you use a long thin cane (3 m, 10 ft) to knock the dew from the grass. You have only to swing this backwards and forwards as you walk over the lawn to see the dew flying off. Such treatment will not only allow earlier mowing but will also help to scatter any worm casts which would otherwise get pushed out by the mower and encourage bare patches in the grass.

Edging

Unless the lawn is edged around with aluminium or plastic edging strip and so does not require it, edging should be done as frequently as mowing. When using edging shears, the best advice I can give is to make sure that the left hand holding the handle which controls the bottom blade is kept still, work only with the right hand and keep moving.

Battery-operated edgers make the job easier and much faster and are worth considering if you have large areas of lawn to cope with. With these I can do the edging in my own garden in less than a quarter of the time it takes with ordinary shears.

Helpful hint

If edging is done regularly there is no necessity to pick up the trimmings, these will shrivel up and go into the soil. But if the trimmings are too long, some will form roots from the joints and start growing and there will be a weedy, ragged edge to the lawn.

Maintaining the lawn

The time for maintaining the lawn – giving it the attention it needs to keep it healthy – is in the autumn as soon as the mowing season has finished.

First, rake over well to get out dead grass, pull up creeping weeds and scratch the soil surface.

After a season of hard wear it is essential to get air to the roots of the plants. Fork over the surface, using an ordinary garden fork and pushing this in to a depth of 5 to 8 cm (2 to 3 in), then bring the handle back until the turf begins to lift and the surface is cracked. An easier alternative is to use a spiked roller or a hollow tine fork. The latter piece of equipment extracts small cores of soil and grass.

Aerating treatment is usually followed by a topdressing with equal parts of peat, fine soil and sand. On a heavy soil, use double the amount of sand, on a light soil, double the amount of peat. Spread this mixture over the lawn by scattering a shovelful to the square metre (yard), and push it about with the back of the rake so it is not left lying about in heaps. When finished, it should be possible to see the grass standing up through it.

Forking the lawn helps to get air to the roots of the grass (*below*). An alternative is to use a special hollow-tine aerator (*right*). Follow this treatment with a topdressing

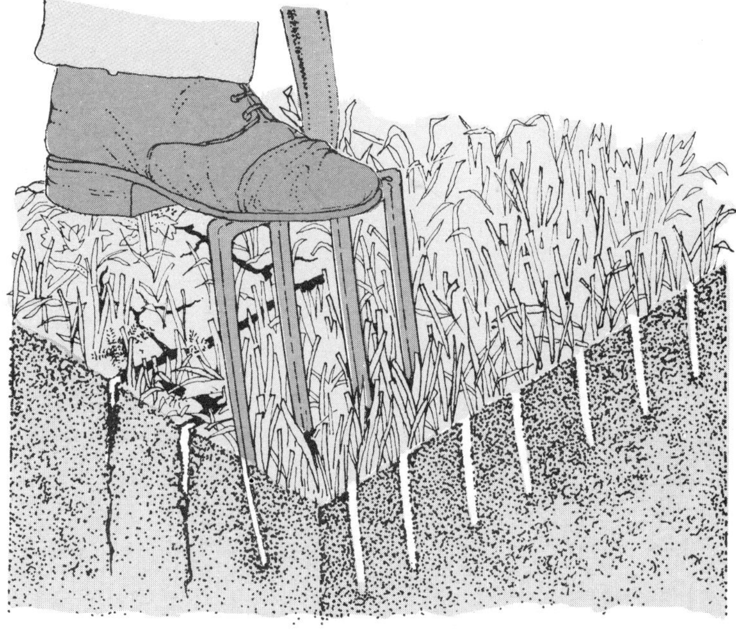

One thing I do not believe in doing is killing worms on the average lawn. This is done on a bowling green, of course, but on the garden lawn I think worms do more good than harm, they help with the drainage, help with aeration of the soil and with the cultivation generally.

Feeding

This is done in the autumn to replace what has been lost during the growing season and I also believe in feeding during the summer months as well in showery weather when there is less likelihood of scorch and the effect is seen more quickly.

There is a range of lawn fertilisers on the market but a general fertiliser will also be all right for the job and will save money.

Helpful hint

However, if there are weeds in the lawn then it is good practice to use a lawn fertiliser with an added selective weedkiller – this saves on time as the weed controlling can be done at the same time as the feeding.

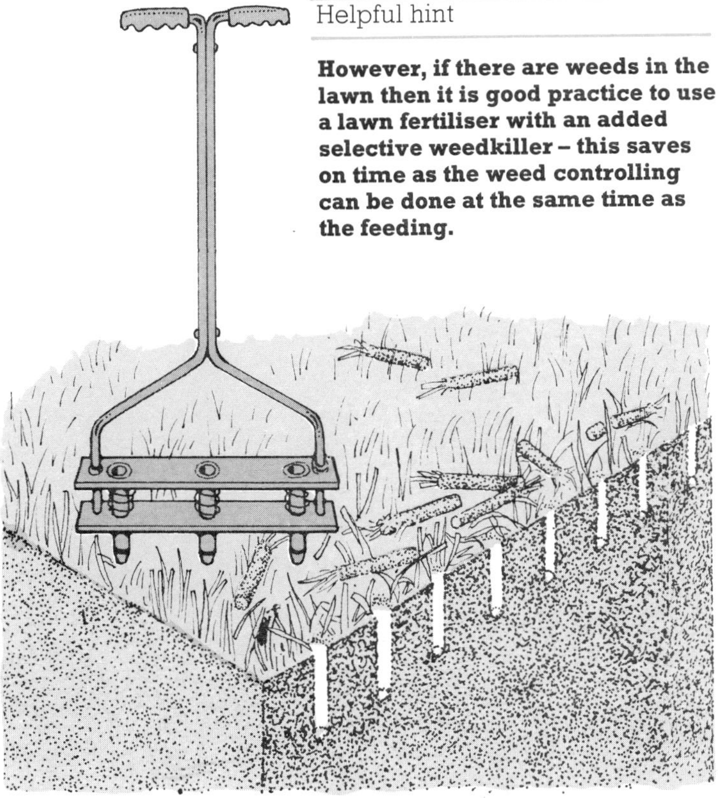

Liquid fertilisers have a swift and marked effect. High in nitrogen, they cause a lot of soft growth which will scorch fast if there is a hot dry spell. If used too late in the summer, the grass is soft during the winter and encourages the spread of fungal and other diseases.

Moss

Moss is one of the most common lawn problems. It excludes air, competes with the grass for light and food. All of which has a bad effect on the grass.

Raking when the weather is damp and mild will spread the moss. Instead apply a mosskiller which can be bought in the form of pellets, granules, dust or liquid and should be applied according to the maker's instructions. Mecurised lawn sand is another useful remedy. Such treatment is most effective in the spring but mosskillers and lawnsand should not be used in dry periods or frosty weather. As moss is usually a problem in shady places or on wet and poorly drained soil, try to improve aeration by spiking and feed the grass to maintain its vigour.

Weeds

These are easy to control these days and do not present a major problem. I never worry when annual seedlings, such as groundsel and chickweed, germinate with the grass seed. As a matter of fact, I like to see them, they act as a nursery crop and provide shelter for the young seedling grass. They usually vanish with the first few mowings and if not they are easily treated with selective weedkillers.

The broad-leaved weeds, buttercups, dandelions, plantains, daisies, spoil the appearance of the lawn. The leaves spread and choke the grass and eventually lead to the development of bare patches in winter if they get too bad.

Selective weedkillers should be applied at the rate recommended.

Lawns and lawn care

To get the best effect from these chemicals both grass and weeds should be in active growth, from late April to early June or in August and September. Avoid hot, dry periods.

Be sure to apply the weedkiller on a still, dry day otherwise any droplets blown about will disfigure plants growing near the lawn edges.

Helpful hint

When using selective weedkiller from a watering can, make sure the can is washed out with hot water and detergent after use. Water from a dirty can will do a lot of damage in the garden. I always keep a special metal can and rose, clearly labelled, for this purpose only.

Droplets of selective weedkillers remain on broad-leaved weeds but run off the grass blades

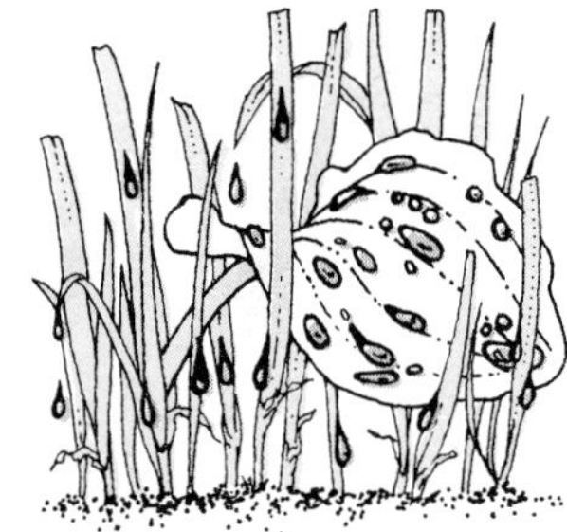

Common lawn weeds
(1) Dandelion (2) Daisy (3) Buttercup (4) Plantain (5) Clover (6) Yarrow (7) Thistle

Patching lawns

To deal with a worn piece of lawn, lay a turf over the bare patch, cut around it with a half-moon cutter, lift the turf within the cut, break up the soil surface with a fork and drop in the turf patch. If you haven't a spare piece of turf, break up the surface and fill the hole with soil and seed.

Alternatively, prick over the worn area with a fork, leaving holes 1 to 2·5 cm (½ to 1 in) apart and 1 cm (½ in) deep. Sprinkle a mixture of fine soil, peat, sand and grass seed over the area and push this into the holes with

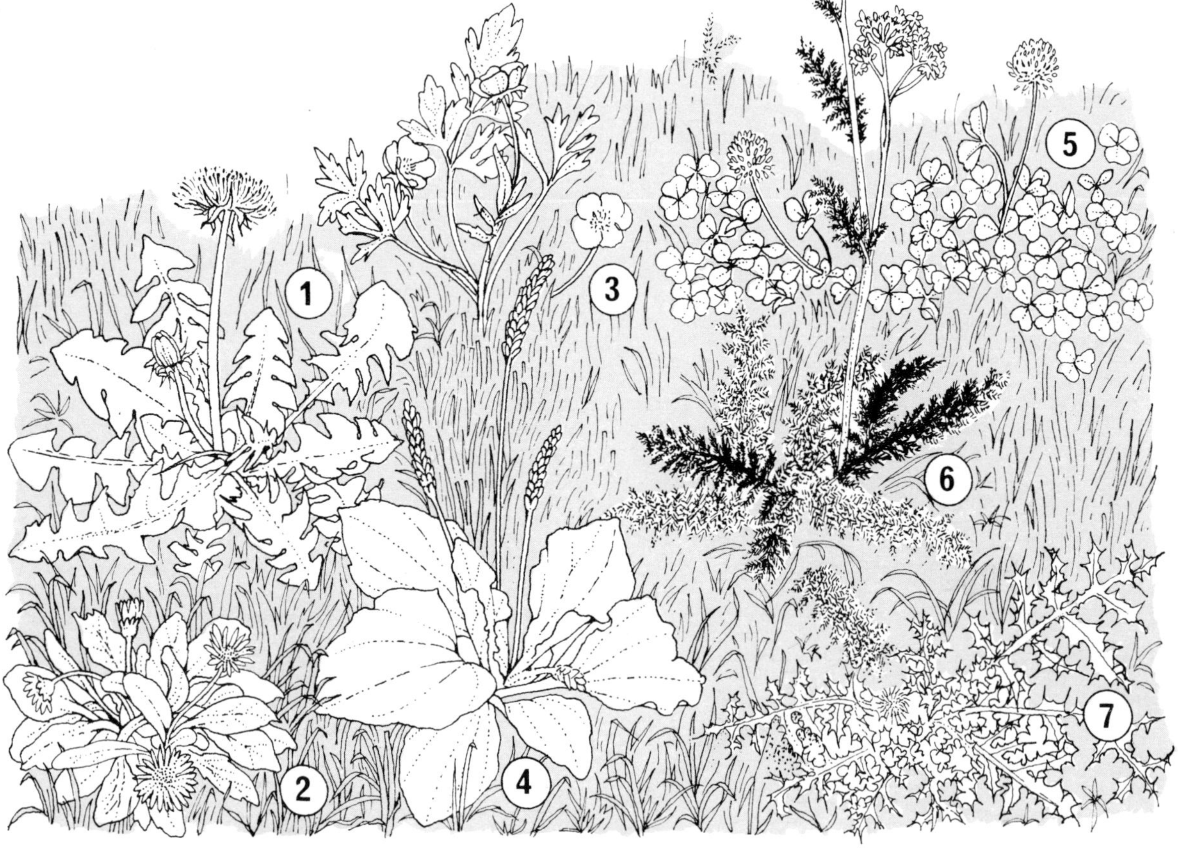

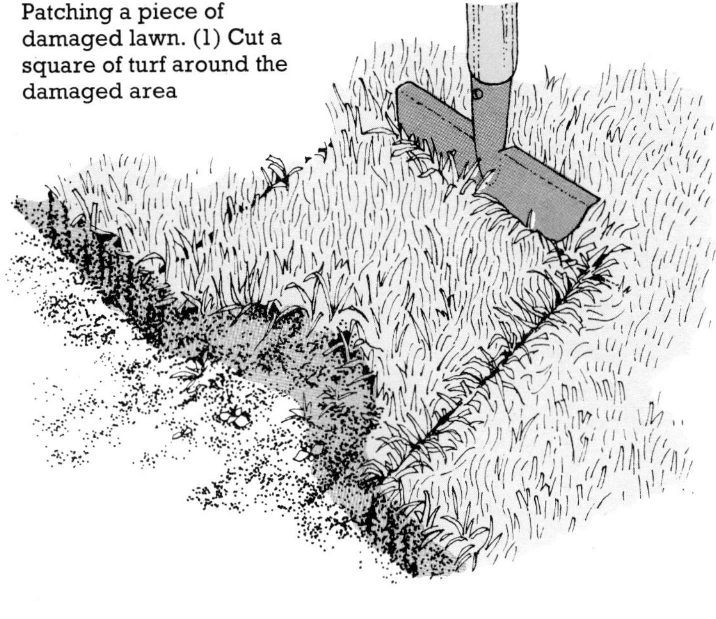

Patching a piece of damaged lawn. (1) Cut a square of turf around the damaged area

(2) Lift and reverse the square. Fill the hole with a mixture of soil and grass seed

the back of a rake. The mixture falls into the holes and little tufts of grass grow which will quickly spread and cover the whole area.

All forms of treatment should be carried out at the same time of the year as lawns are sown or turfed.

If there are patches in the lawn, you should ask yourself why they are there. Is it natural wear and tear? Have you used the fertiliser incorrectly – too concentrated or in hot, dry spells? Are there a lot of weeds? Are there high patches where the bottom blades of the mower are scraping? If this is the problem these areas of grass should be lifted and some soil removed from underneath.

Watering

Like any plant, grass goes brown when the soil gets dry. During periods of hot, dry weather give sufficient water to soak in a couple of inches. The easiest way of applying water is to use a sprinkler which will assure good, even coverage.

Helpful hint

Treat dry, brown patches with water to which a few drops of washing up liquid have been added. The detergent will prevent surface run off and help the water to soak into very dry soil.

Chamomile lawn

This is sometimes suggested as an alternative to a grass lawn, but I've yet to see one that I would feel proud of and would like to have in my own garden. They are not easy to maintain even if you do get the plants established, they require hand weeding as selective weedkillers cannot be used and there is never sufficient cover to give the green velvet carpet-like effect of grass.

Starting plants

A garden isn't a garden without plants and these days stocking the garden can be an expensive business. There are ways of cutting the costs, although you may have to wait longer to see the results.

Colourful annuals and a wide range of vegetables are easily grown from seed and many favourite shrubs, trees and fruit can be grown from cuttings. Most gardeners are generous and will let you have snippings from plants and pieces of overgrown clumps.

Follow a few simple rules and you should achieve the success and satisfaction of raising a lot of your own plants.

Seed Sowing

Out of doors

1 The first essential is to make the seedbed properly. If the soil is heavy, dig it in the autumn and leave in large lumps for the frost to break down.

2 Before sowing make the bed firm by treading over it and then rake the surface to get stones out of the way and to break the soil down to a fine crumbly texture. Sprinkle on a general garden fertiliser at the rate of 55 g to the sq m (2 oz to the sq yd).

3 All seed should be sown thinly to avoid waste of seed and time spent in thinning. When dealing with very fine seed such as that of carrot it is helpful to mix it with sand and sow the mixture, this makes for a more even distribution.

Pelletted seeds are seeds which have been surrounded with a hard soluble coat of a clay-like material. This makes the seed larger and enables easier and more accurate sowing. However, they are more expensive to buy and in a dry season there may not be sufficient moisture to soak through the outer coating as well as the seed coating to allow germination to take place. On the whole, I don't think there is anything better than using seed in the ordinary way.

Sowing vegetables

When sowing vegetable seed allow sufficient space between the rows to give the vegetable room to develop.

Making a drill for small seeds with the edge of a hoe (1). For larger seeds, use the full width of the hoe to take out the drill (2)

Take out a drill as shown, try to make it an even depth all the way along, and water it well. Sprinkle the seed thinly along the drill and gently push the soil back with the hoe. There should be sufficient moisture to last until the seed germinates. Seeds vary in the time it takes them to germinate. This depends on the warmth of the soil as well as on the type of seed.

When the seedlings are a few inches high, thin out if necessary to leave the required distance between them.

Left When thinning seedlings place a finger on each side of the one which is to remain to keep it firm.
Above After thinning firm in by treading gently down each side of the row

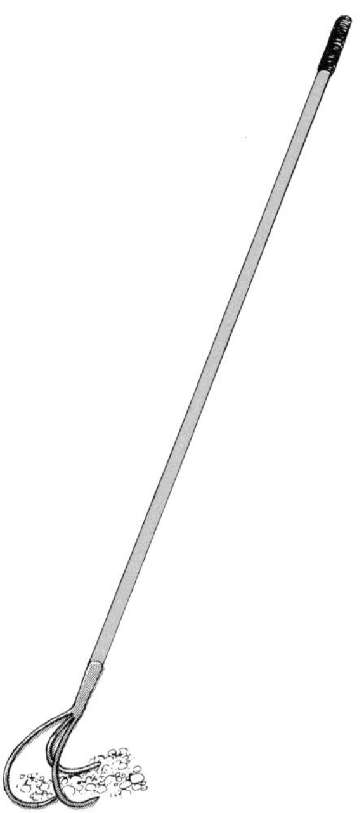

Above A three-pronged cultivator is a useful tool for controlling weeds and breaking up the soil surface

Look to the season ahead and do not do all your sowing of the same crop at the same time. This will be a waste because subsequently all the crops come in together. Parsnips must be sown early; peas should be sown in batches; sow lettuce every three weeks and only a quarter row at a time, the thinnings from the quarter row can be transplanted to crop 10 to 14 days later. Radish should be sown thinly and only a metre (yard) or so at a time as they soon bolt.

Sowing annuals

If the garden is weedy, it is advisable to sow flower seeds in drills as well so that the ground can be hoed and the weeds kept down. Otherwise, make the bed firm, rake it well to get a fine, even surface, and with a pointed stick mark out an irregular pattern like a jigsaw.

Label each patch and then sprinkle the appropriate seeds over the surface and lightly rake them in.

Bird protection

There is an old saying about seed sowing which has a lot of truth behind it:

One for the pigeon and one for the crow,
One to rot, and one to grow.

Apart from sowing more seeds than you need, the only totally satisfactory way to keep the birds off the seeds is to use nets or cotton to cover the seeded areas.

Protection from mice entails the use of baits but these must be placed under tiles or inside pieces of drainpipe where birds and domestic animals can't reach them.

Helpful hint

Never sow too early. The hedgerows are the best barometers I know: when they come into leaf it is an indication that the soil temperature is rising and sowing can begin. Many seeds are lost through sowing too early in a fine spell in January or February; this is invariably followed by more cold and wet weather and the seeds decay.

Using a hoe correctly. *Left* When operating a draw hoe the user walks forwards. *Right* When operating a Dutch hoe the user walks backwards

Starting plants

Sowing times

Early spring Sow as soon as the hedgerows show green.

Broad beans, beetroot, leaf beet, broccoli, Brussels sprouts, carrots, leeks, lettuce, onions, parsnips, peas, radish, spinach, turnips.

Hardy annuals and perennials.

Late spring Sow at the time of the last expected frost.

French beans, runner beans, spring cabbage, kale, cauliflower, marrow, swede.

Half-hardy annuals and perennials.

Under glass

This is a valuable way of getting some of the tender plants off to an early start if you have a greenhouse or heated frame. Sowing seeds in the house is not so successful but if you have a light window in a warm room it is worth a try.

Seed sowing indoors. (1) Fill the tray with compost. (2) Level off with a piece of board. (3) Firm evenly and then water using a fine rose on the can. (4) Make holes for large seeds with a pencil or dibber. (5) Cover the seed with fine soil to a depth the size of the seed

Most will take an average of two months to mature and as planting out is usually done after the last expected frost (late May) it is important not to start the plants too early. Leave it until March and then use a propagating frame where it is more economical to maintain a higher temperature (10 to 15°C, 50 to 60°F) within a smaller space.

The method Using a seed-sowing compost such as John Innes or one of the peat-based kinds, fill the boxes or pots, making the compost moderately firm and perfectly even on the surface. Water well an hour or so before you sow the seed and it should not be necessary to water again until the seedlings come up. Sow the seed thinly over the surface.

Helpful hint

When dealing with fine seed such as that of lobelia, streptocarpus, gloxinia and begonias, put the seeds on a square of white paper which has been folded down the middle. This will act as a channel from which the seeds can be shaken.

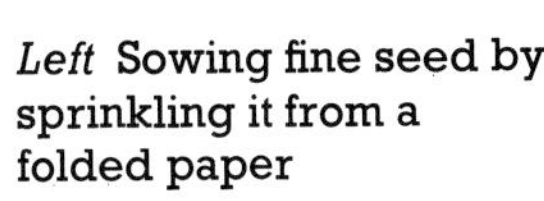

Left Sowing fine seed by sprinkling it from a folded paper

Little or no covering of compost is needed over fine seeds, but sprinkle a quarter inch or so over larger seeds such as those of French and African marigolds and salvias.

Put a sheet of glass over the top to prevent loss of moisture and a sheet of newspaper over that to provide shade from the sun.

Peat pots Trays of peat pots are useful for seed sowing and the great joy of these is that there is no need to disturb the seedling roots: the complete pot can be transplanted and the roots will eventually grow out through the pot. They are especially good for growing cucumbers, melons, marrow, runner and broad beans, peas and tomatoes.

Germinating difficult seeds In order for the young shoot and root to emerge, the seed must absorb water and with some of the hard-coated seeds this takes a long time. Speed up the process by rubbing the outside of the seed with a piece of emery paper; this scratches the surface and enables water to be absorbed faster.

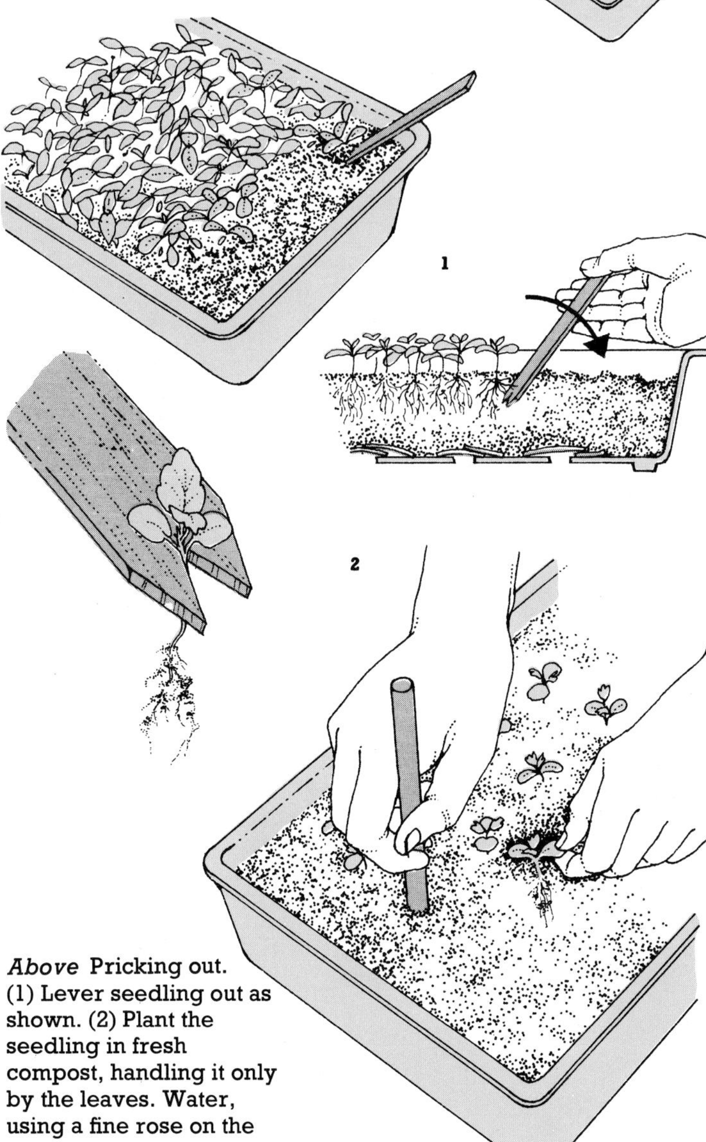

Above Pricking out. (1) Lever seedling out as shown. (2) Plant the seedling in fresh compost, handling it only by the leaves. Water, using a fine rose on the watering can

Care of seedlings

As soon as the seedlings come up, take off the glass and newspaper and put the boxes or pots in the lightest possible position.

When watering, always use a fine rose on the can.

Move the seedlings (pricking out) before they get overcrowded or drawn.

Starting plants

Cuttings

When you look enviously at shrubs and plants in a friend's garden, go one step further and ask for a small piece of the young growth. Kept moist and treated as suggested here you may be surprised at how successful you can be in growing plants from cuttings, but only use healthy material from vigorous plants.

There are three main types of cuttings: softwood, half-ripe and hardwood.

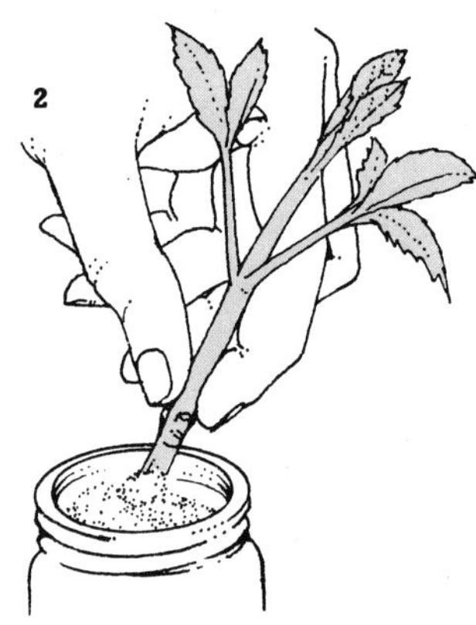

(2) Dip the base of the prepared cutting in hormone rooting powder

Softwood cuttings.
(1) Trim off the lower leaves and cut the stem below a joint or node

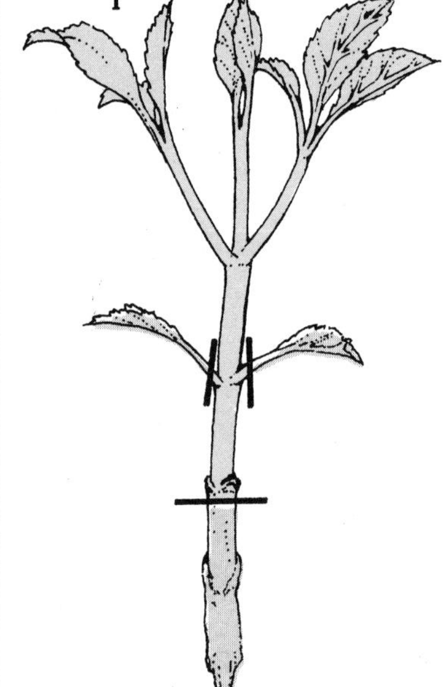

(3) Insert the cuttings in pots, or boxes, of sandy compost

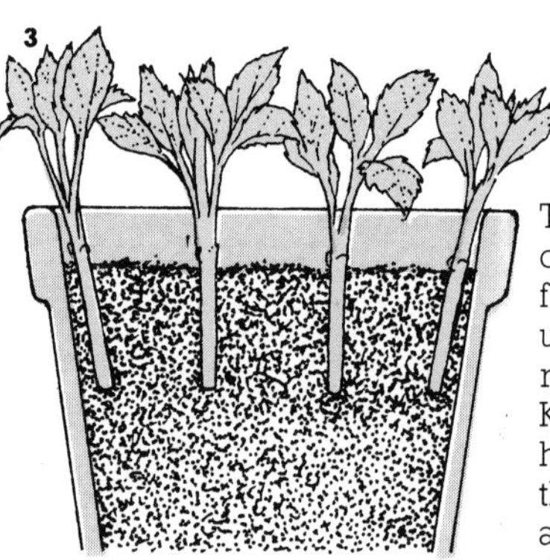

Softwood cuttings

These are taken in spring or early summer from soft shoots which can be easily snapped off. They should be 8 or 10 cm (3 or 4 in) long and have the lower leaves removed and be cut across immediately below a joint. Dip the base in hormone rooting powder and insert the stem in a pot or box filled with sandy rooting compost. This is the method to use for plants such as geranium, coleus, fuchsia, chrysanthemum and dahlia.

(4) Place the pot inside a plastic bag and seal the top. This helps to minimise water loss

The most critical factor in the rooting of cuttings is to stop loss of moisture from the leaves as much as possible until new roots are formed to take in replacement moisture from the soil. Keeping the top growth damp will help to stop water evaporating from the leaves and this is the reason why a layer of polythene film placed over the cuttings is beneficial – the moisture collects under it and creates a humid atmosphere around the cuttings. Once signs of growth are seen the cuttings can be potted up.

Bottom heat If the temperature of the soil can be maintained at about 21°C (70°F) softwood cuttings will root much more rapidly. This can be achieved by using a propagating frame with some form of bottom heat – soil-warming cables, electric light bulbs or by placing a specially constructed propagator over a radiator.

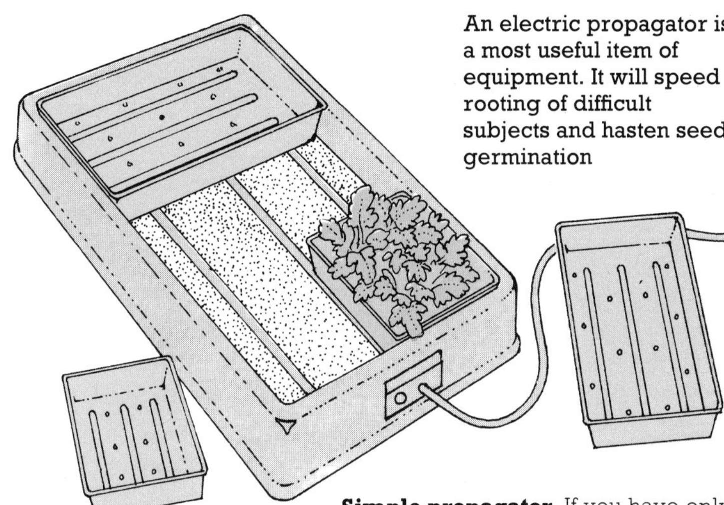

An electric propagator is a most useful item of equipment. It will speed rooting of difficult subjects and hasten seed germination

Helpful hint

Prevent cuttings from flagging by keeping them in a close, humid atmosphere and they will root more quickly.

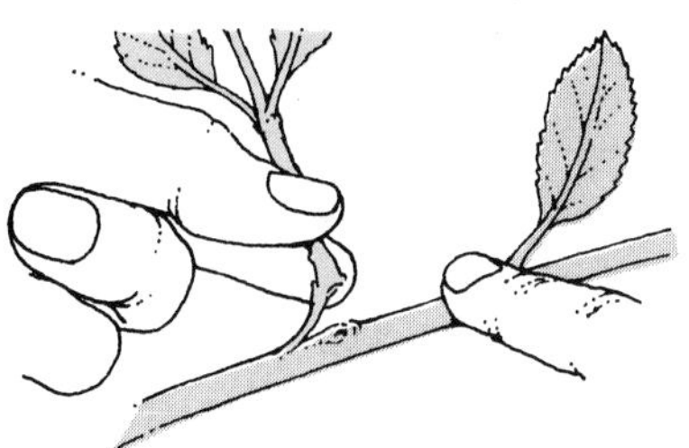

Half-ripe cuttings. Tear the cuttings from the mother plant with a strip of old wood

The strip of old wood is known as a heel

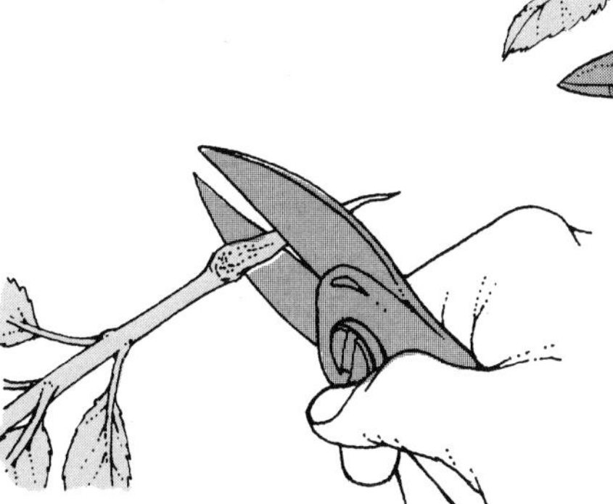

Trim the heel with secateurs or a sharp knife

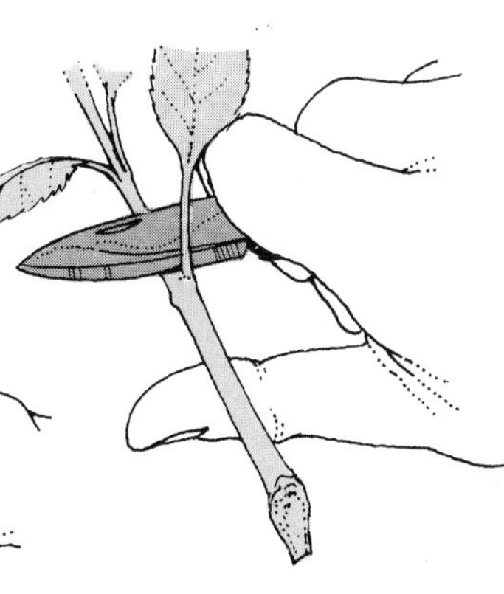

Remove the lower leaves, then dip the end in rooting powder and insert in a pot or box

Simple propagator If you have only a few cuttings to root, there is no need to go to the expense of buying a propagator. Insert the cuttings in a pot, place this inside a polythene bag and seal the top. Keep in a light, warm place but not in full sun. A similar atmosphere can be created by using a plastic pot cover.

Half-ripe cuttings

These are cuttings taken in summer from shoots which have begun to turn woody at the base. They are from 5 to 10 cm (2 to 4 in) long and may be taken with a heel of the old wood.

Dip the base of the cuttings in hormone rooting powder and insert them in sandy soil in a cold frame or in a pot which is placed inside a polythene bag. Keep shaded from the sun. As before, once signs of new growth can be seen the cuttings can be removed and potted up individually. This is a good method for most shrubs.

Hardwood cuttings

For most people, these are the easiest kind of cutting to root. They are taken in autumn when the wood is ripe from firm one-year-old stems. Make the cutting 23 to 30 cm (9 to 12 in) long and trim off below a bud or joint. I find it helps if a little of the bark is scraped off at the bottom, the base dipped into water and then into hormone rooting powder and excess shaken off. The cuttings are then inserted to half their depth in sand in a trench in a sheltered part of the garden and made firm.

Shoots will form from the cuttings in spring and in the following autumn the young plants can be dug out and replanted. A good method for use on all shrubs and bush and cane fruits.

Hardwood cuttings. Trim the top of the cutting to just above a joint (or node) and the bottom to below a joint (*right*). Remove any side shoots

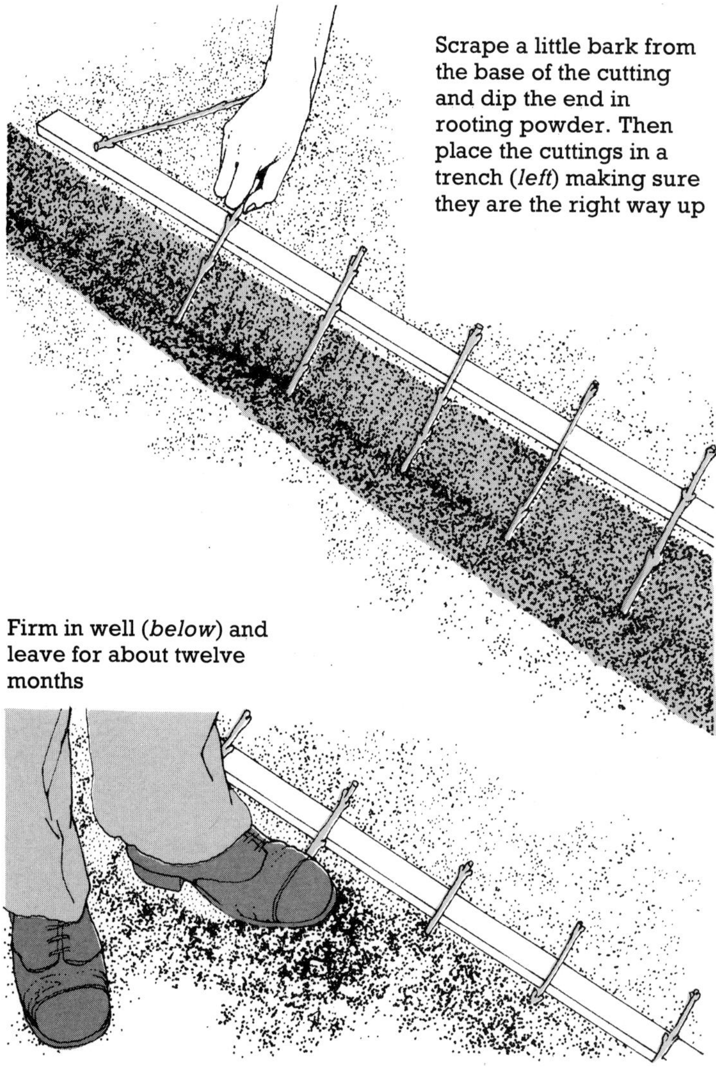

Scrape a little bark from the base of the cutting and dip the end in rooting powder. Then place the cuttings in a trench (*left*) making sure they are the right way up

Firm in well (*below*) and leave for about twelve months

Potting plants

Potting is the process by which plants are placed in pots or are moved on from one pot to another. It is a procedure used for most seedlings and cuttings and all plants grown indoors.

There are three main stages in the process:

1 The term potting off or potting up is applied to seedlings or cuttings when they are moved from the pots or boxes in which they were started off. This should be done before the seedlings have become spindly or elongated. Cuttings are potted up as soon as they have formed roots, which is indicated by signs of new leaf growth.

2 Potting on is used to describe the transferring of a plant from one pot to a larger one. This takes place when a plant fills its existing pot with roots and is said to be potbound. When this happens, roots will grow through the drainage holes and on knocking the plant from the pot the outside of the rootball is seen to be covered with a web of roots.

3 Repotting refers to the annual potting of permanent indoor or greenhouse plants which are usually replaced in pots of the same size. This allows for the replacement and renewal of some of the growing mixture.

1

Repotting. First, water the plant, then remove it from its pot by banging the edge on a hard surface

2

The potting compost Under no circumstances should ordinary garden soil be used for potting. It usually packs down too hard, and may contain pests and diseases and possibly an earthworm or two which will cause havoc to the root system. Instead, invest in a ready mixed potting compost, either a soil-based one such as the John Innes mixes, or one of the many peat-based composts. All of these contain fertiliser and the John Innes mixes are available in four strengths: seed compost, No 1, No 2 and No 3, with the fertiliser content increasing with the number.

Seed compost is used for cuttings and seedlings, No 1 for small plants, No 2 for plants in the middle size pots and No 3 for repotting the more woody plants.

The method The pots should be clean, free from all traces of old compost and roots, and clay pots must be supplied with drainage material, usually a piece of broken pot which is placed so that the concave side is over the drainage hole. There is no need to put drainage material into plastic pots.

The plant to be potted should have been previously watered so that it can be removed with ease.

After potting, water well and keep the plants in shade and a fairly close atmosphere for a few days, after which they can be returned to their normal growing conditions.

When repotting, the procedure is more or less the same except that as much of the old compost as possible is removed from between the roots with a sharp stick or the fingers, but this must be done without causing too much damage to the roots. The plant is then replaced in a clean pot and fresh compost is worked in around the roots.

Above Place the root ball in a larger pot and (*left*) fill in with potting compost to just above the original soil level. Firm so that there are no air pockets and then water

Shopping, planting and aftercare

These days, a garden centre is the best place to go to when you need plants or equipment for the garden. Here you can wander at leisure, see plants you don't know by name and get advice from the experienced staff on how tall they grow, what kind of soil they need and where they should be planted.

All good garden centres carry a wide range of garden sundries, too, and you should be able to find everything you need from plant ties to weedkiller.

When buying plants, remember that those growing in containers will be easier to get established than those with bare roots.

One other point, if shopping in warm weather, get your purchases home quickly before they have a chance to get overheated in the car.

The garden shop is another in-valuable if smaller source of chemi-cals, seeds, bedding plants and equipment.

If you have a neither a garden centre or shop in your locality, many of the large nursery firms run a mail order business.

In many areas there are local Allotment Societies which you can join even if you do not have an allotment. They buy in bulk, and certain fertilisers and plants such as tomatoes and bedding plants can be purchased cheaply from them.

Tools

When buying tools the important point to remember is that you get what you pay for. If you buy a good tool it will last a long time. Buy a cheap tool and it will be disappoint-ing: not so easy to handle and won't last nearly as long.

The essential garden tools are a good spade, a good fork, a rake, a hoe and a trowel. Check the weight, size and balance of the spade and fork, you will have to use both for long periods, so they must feel comfortable to handle. This is likely to be a problem if several members of the family will be using the tool – the full-sized version may be too heavy. There are several kinds of hoe but the Dutch hoe is the most useful, again make sure that it is light enough for you to use for an hour or so at a time.

Other tools and equipment can be bought as and when you want them. Secateurs, shears, a lawn mower and edging shears will probably come high on the list, together with more minor paraphenalia such as a knife, string, labels, watering can or hose and canes for support.

Maintenance Clean all tools after use and, if possible, hang them up. If they are not made of stainless steel it is particularly important to follow the cleaning procedure – wash off the soil, let the tool dry and then wipe it over with an oily cloth.

Shears and secateurs should be dried after use and all the moveable parts given an occasional oiling.

How to treat newly acquired plants

Container grown These plants can be planted at any time of the year, even when they are in flower.

1 Water the plants well before removing them from their con-tainers.

2 Dig a hole twice as wide as the root ball.

3 Never plant too deeply – the top of the root ball should be just below the soil surface.

4 Mix some organic matter – peat, ground bark, decayed manure – into the soil before returning it around the root ball and firming well.

5 Water thoroughly and water again in 3 to 4 days if the weather remains dry.

Soak the container-grown plant before planting

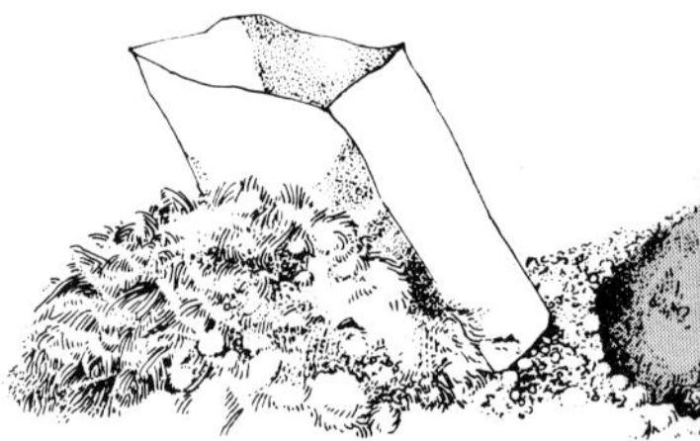

Dig a hole and fork compost and fertiliser into the bottom

Position the plant so that the top of the root ball is just below the surface

Shopping, planting and aftercare

Cut away the container with a sharp knife

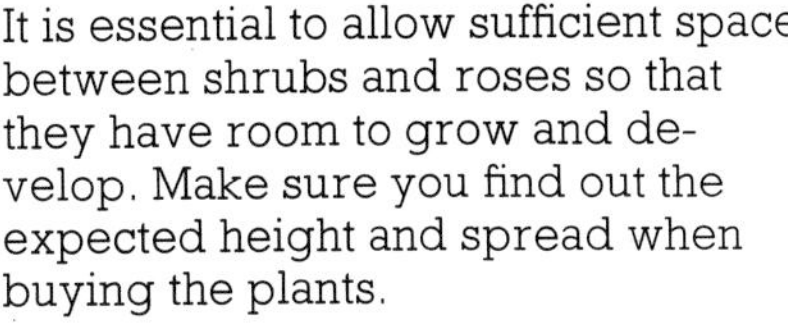

It is essential to allow sufficient space between shrubs and roses so that they have room to grow and develop. Make sure you find out the expected height and spread when buying the plants.

Bare-rooted These are usually deciduous plants and the main planting season is from November to March.

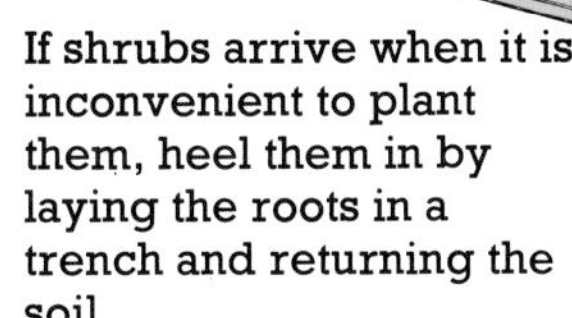

If shrubs arrive when it is inconvenient to plant them, heel them in by laying the roots in a trench and returning the soil

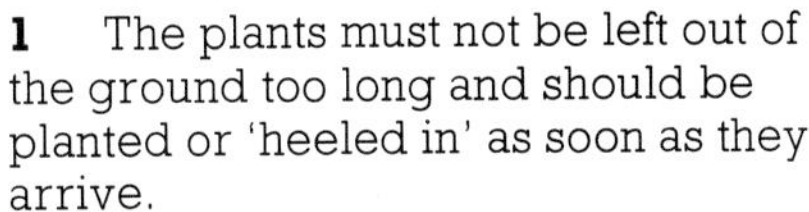

1 The plants must not be left out of the ground too long and should be planted or 'heeled in' as soon as they arrive.

2 If the roots appear dry, soak them in water for a few hours.

3 Take out a hole wide enough to allow the roots to be fully spread out and deep enough to make sure that the old soil mark on the stem will be slightly below ground level.

4 Fork over the bottom of the hole, and place the shrub in position, spreading its roots well. Add some organic matter to the soil which has been removed and gradually fill in the hole, shaking the shrub occasionally to make sure the soil fills the spaces around the roots. Using the full weight of your body, firm in well.

Return the soil and firm well

Planting a bare-rooted tree. (1) Mark out a circular hole that is larger than the roots when these are spread out. (2) Spread the roots (3) and return the soil

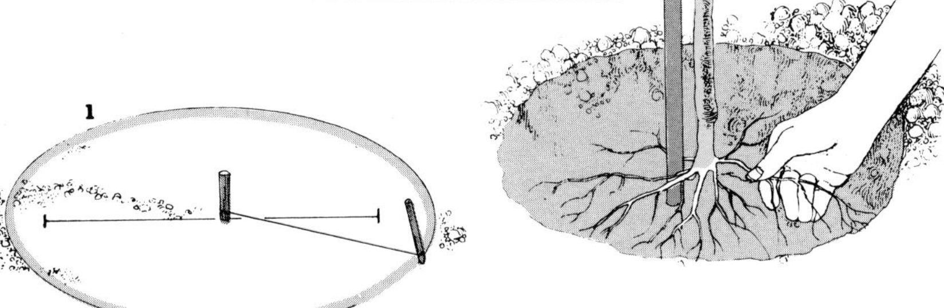

Shopping, planting and aftercare

Planting a balled plant. Place the plant in the hole and then untie the wrapping

Balled plants This is the usual way in which conifers are offered for sale. Planting should be done in autumn or spring.

1 Take out a hole wide enough and deep enough to accommodate the balled roots. Watch the soil mark on the stem and make sure that this is positioned slightly below ground.

2 Place the plant in position, cut the string holding the wrapping in place and roll the wrapping down – there is no need to remove it.

3 Fill in around the balled roots with a mixture of soil and organic matter, making this firm as you go.

4 Water well.

Aftercare If the weather is dry, spray newly planted trees, shrubs with water. Do this at least once a day; it reduces loss of water from the leaves, freshens up the plants and encourages them to root into the soil.

Many of the failures with newly planted shrubs is a result of planting too deeply or a lack of water after planting.

Staking and supporting

All trees should be given a supporting stake to hold them firm against wind rock until the roots have established themselves. When planting a tree which needs support, the stake must be put into the hole before the tree is positioned to prevent any damage to the roots. The stake should be driven about 15 cm (6 in) into the base of the hole so that it is firmly anchored.

Supporting ties between the stake and tree may be the specially made plastic tree ties which have an inbuilt cushion to prevent chafing. If ordinary tarred twine or cord is used there must be a piece of sacking placed between the stake and stem. The tie should be placed almost at the top of the stake, and, for trees, two ties should be used otherwise the young trunk may buckle.

Staking a tree. The stake is positioned first and then the tree. One or more supporting ties will be needed (*below*)

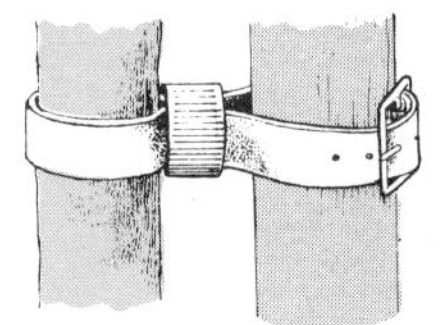

Staking perennials For this job, I use old pea sticks which I push in around the plants. Eventually the plants grow up through the sticks and get all the support they need. Some plants, such as hollyhocks and delphiniums, need individual stakes but try always to make the stakes or canes insignificant, and not too big.

Metal stakes are strong and there is a range of metal and plastic 'canes' available for the purpose. If you find pea sticks difficult to come by, there are special adjustable metal rings which will serve the same purpose.

Moving established plants

First, be guided by the season, November to March is the normal time, although some fruit trees can be lifted in October. Conifers and evergreens should be planted or moved in October and November and from late March to early May.

Some shrubs are easy to move: rhododendrons for example. Dig around the plant with a fork first to find out how far the roots have gone. Then, using a spade, dig underneath and right round and it is usually possible to lift the plant with a good ball of soil because of the close fibrous nature of the roots.

Moving large trees or shrubs is a job for two people. Make a circular

Shopping, planting and aftercare

trench 30 to 60 cm (12 to 24 in) away from the stem, cutting through the thicker roots. Do this a few months before lifting to encourage fibrous roots to form in the ball immediately around the stem and you are more likely to lift it successfully.

This also applies to conifers: chop to the depth of a spade around the conifer a few weeks or a month or two before lifting and this will again encourage fibrous roots to form.

Whatever is being transplanted, it is essential to have a hole ready in the new position so that the lifted plant can be got into the ground in a minimum amount of time.

Protecting plants

Loss of newly planted or transplanted conifers can be explained by the fact that the plants loose moisture from the leaves faster than they can take it up through the roots because of injury caused by root disturbance. This results in the leaves going brown and the plant then dies. One way of preventing the loss of moisture is to cover the plant with a large polythene bag which is tied around the base of the stem and left in position until spring.

Helpful hint

Some plants don't take kindly to being moved: clematis and vines are two widely grown examples, also brooms, genista and gorse. These should always be bought as pot-grown specimens because, when planted from pots, there is little or no disturbance to the roots.

Another way of preventing loss of moisture is to spray the tree over with a sealing solution known as S600; this prevents loss of moisture from the leaves. Incidentally, it can also be used on Christmas trees and will help to prevent needle drop and the tiresome chore of cleaning up.

(1) *Left* Trees must be moved carefully. First use a spade then a fork to tease out as much of the root system as possible. Some of the stronger roots may have to be cut through

(2) *Right* Sacking is used to carry the tree to its new position, where a planting hole has already been prepared, to prevent the roots from drying out

(3) *Left* The roots must be gently spread out and the hole may have to be made larger to accommodate them. It is important that the tree is planted to the same depth as before

(4) *Right* After staking securely, fine soil is worked around the roots and well firmed. The tree is then watered

Pruning

This can be a complicated business and it is important to realise what pruning is intended to accomplish and how.

Why prune?

1 To keep plants shapely and of a reasonable size, and to allow air to circulate freely, by removing overcrowded shoots and straggly, untidy branches.

2 To remove dead, diseased and decayed wood.

3 To redirect growth by encouraging buds to grow in the direction required.

4 To encourage new growth. Cutting back the plant will force it into more growth production, but it must be done judiciously.

5 To help the formation of flowers and fruit by retaining the right sort of bud. Removal of dead flower heads is important as many plants direct their energies into seed production.

To achieve its purpose pruning involves the removal of shoot tips and, in some cases, the whole or part of the stem.

By removing any part of the shoot, you stimulate growth from the buds lower down the stem. In some cases, a number of the lower buds will start growing to form side shoots, in others only the bud immediately below the cut will grow to form a shoot.

Annuals are good examples of plants which will produce a number of side shoots to make good-looking bushy plants.

Roses, on the other hand, generally produce one shoot only from the bud immediately below the cut. Cut to a bud which is going to grow in the right direction – away from the centre of the plant.

As a general rule, the more severe the pruning the more vigorous will the resulting growth be.

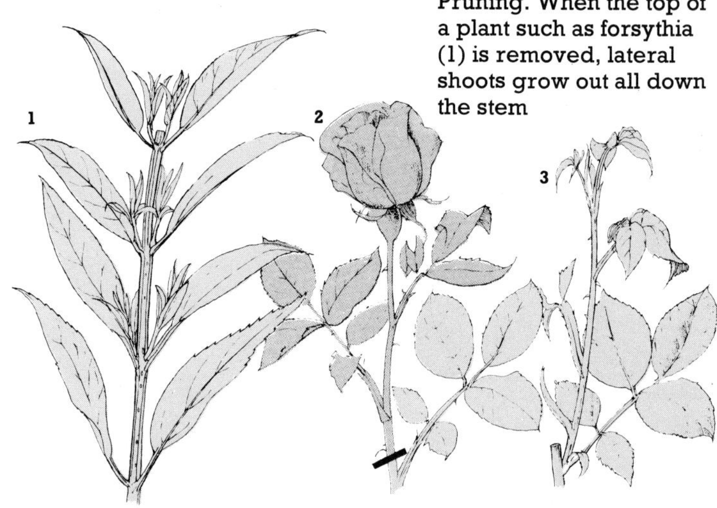

Pruning. When the top of a plant such as forsythia (1) is removed, lateral shoots grow out all down the stem

Above right **When the top of a rose is removed, however (2), only the bud immediately below the cut grows out (3)**

Above **Pinching out the top of an annual encourages the growth of side shoots**

Tools

The basic equipment for pruning consists of a good pair of secateurs and a sharp knife. There are many sorts of secateurs available and you should choose a model which fits your hand – too heavy and large a pair will cause wrist and hand fatigue. For cutting thicker branches a pruning saw is essential and most of those made for pruning cut when you pull rather than push the blade.

If you have to deal with tall trees, you will need a long-handled cutter on a 2·5, 3, 3·5 m (8, 10, or 12 ft) stem, and for pruning high and heavy branches there are tree loppers, about 60 cm (2 ft) long and with powerful jaws. Keep a tin of sealing compound such as Stockholm tar or Arbrex handy to paint over large wounds.

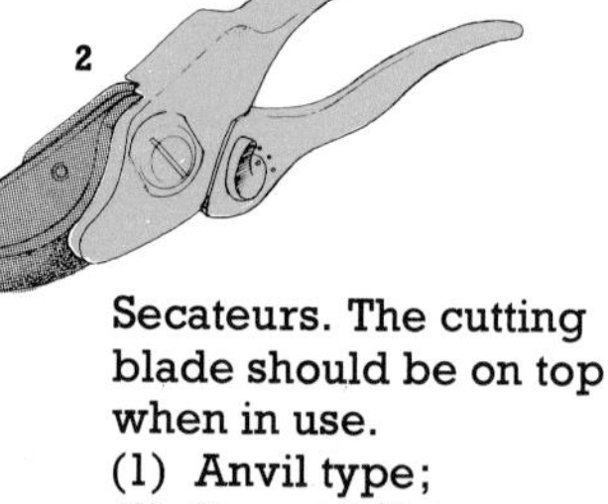

Secateurs. The cutting blade should be on top when in use.
(1) Anvil type;
(2) Parrot-bill type

How to prune

Always cut the stem cleanly, either immediately above a bud or above a healthy side shoot. If a whole shoot is to be removed this should be done so that no stub remains. Large cuts should be painted over with a sealing compound to prevent the entry of disease organisms.

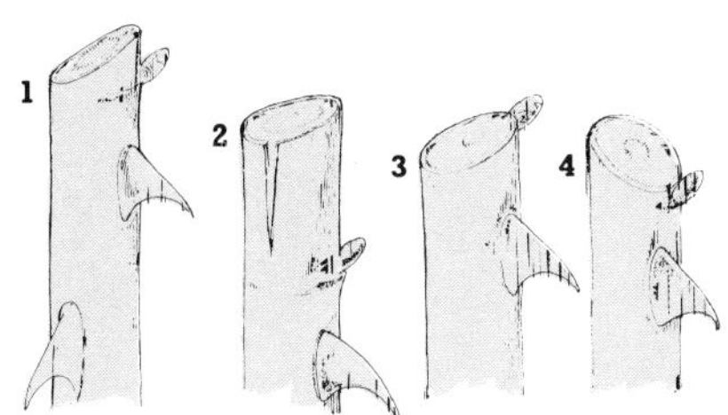

It is important that pruning cuts are correctly positioned.
(1) Correct.
(2) Too far above a bud.
(3) Too close to a bud.
(4) Slanting the wrong way

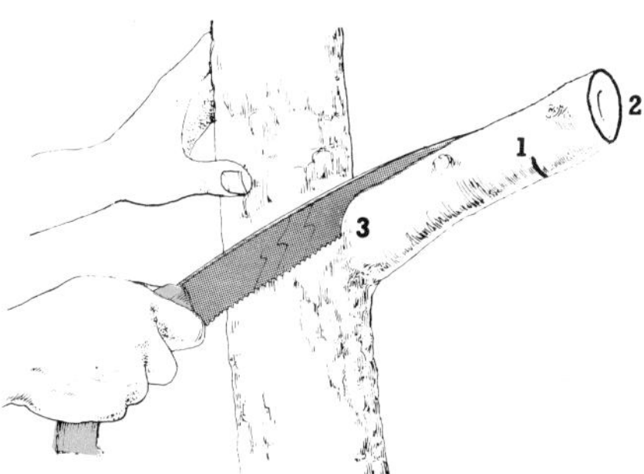

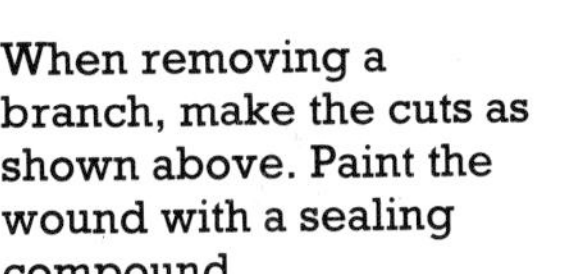

When removing a branch, make the cuts as shown above. Paint the wound with a sealing compound

What to prune

Golden rule: Many plants are spoiled by overpruning. Too much pruning causes vigorous growth which is often at the expense of flower and fruit production. If in doubt, *don't prune*.

Trees require little or no pruning except for an occasional thinning of the branches and the removal of dead and diseased wood. However, trained trees, such as cordon and espalier-trained fruit trees, must be pruned to keep the size and shape correct and to bring about the formation of the fruit buds.

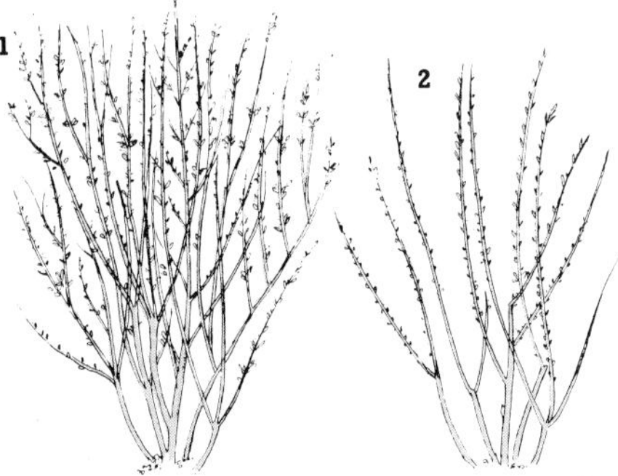

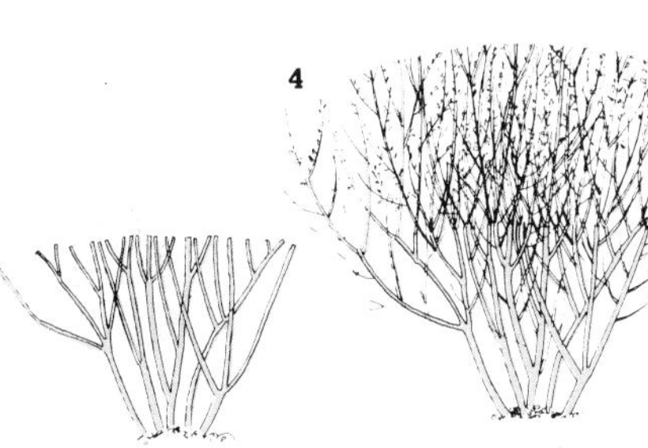

Pruning must be done correctly to keep the natural shape. (1) Shrub before pruning. (2) Shrub correctly pruned. (3) Shrub incorrectly pruned by being chopped across. This results in bushy, top-heavy growth (4)

Pruning shrubs that flower in autumn and late summer. (1) Before. (2) In early spring cut back close to the base.

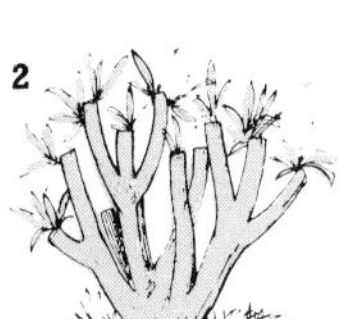

Deciduous shrubs vary in their pruning requirements, many tend to get overgrown and too dense without some thinning. Most shrubs fall into one of the following groups:

A Those that flower in late summer and early autumn on growth produced in the current year are pruned in March. These will usually stand fairly hard pruning provided it is done early enough to give as long as possible for new growth to be produced before the shrubs flower.

Pruning

B Those that flower in spring and early summer are pruned immediately flowering is finished to encourage the production of new branches in late summer and autumn which will provide the flowers the following year. Cut back only the growth which has flowered to sturdy young shoots lower down the stem. Similar pruning is used for the winter and early-spring-flowering shrubs.

C Those that flower on spurs on the older branches are pruned in winter to keep them within bounds and prevent overcrowding.

Evergreen shrubs seldom need pruning unless they are grown as a formal or clipped hedge. If growth becomes very dense or uneven, cut out the occasional branch when the flowering is over.

Rhododendrons only require the removal of dead flowers. Trailing shrubs such as the heathers will be more compact if trimmed over with shears in early spring.

Climbing plants The pruning of these depends on the amount of space available. Routine cutting out of dead wood and thinning of overcrowded growth may be all that is required. However, if restricted wall space demands more rigorous cutting back, then the pruning rules are the same as those given for deciduous shrubs: those that flower from midsummer onwards being pruned in early spring, those flowering in spring and early summer being pruned immediately flowering is finished.

The vines and other climbers grown for their foliage are pruned in winter if deciduous and early spring if evergreen.

Roses are pruned when the bushes are dormant, generally between January and March, the milder the climate, the earlier the pruning should be done before the bushes start to produce new shoots.

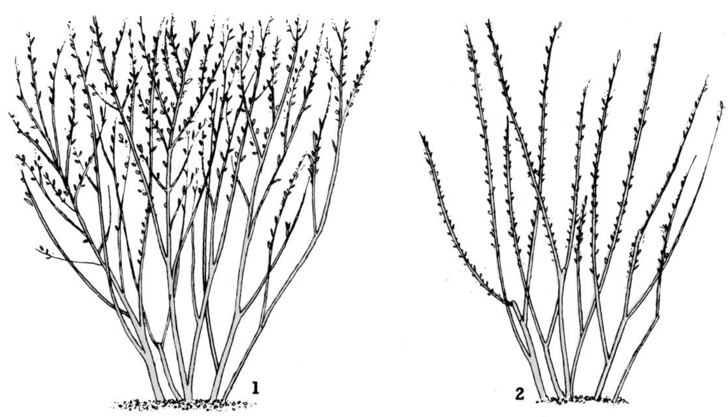

Above **Pruning spring-flowering shrubs. (1) Before. (2) After flowering, cut back the shoots which have flowered**

Some shrubs, such as lilac, roses, azaleas and rhododendrons produce shoots around the base of the stems which grow from below ground. Remove these suckers carefully by pushing away the soil to expose the base and then pulling or cutting them off, see page 53.

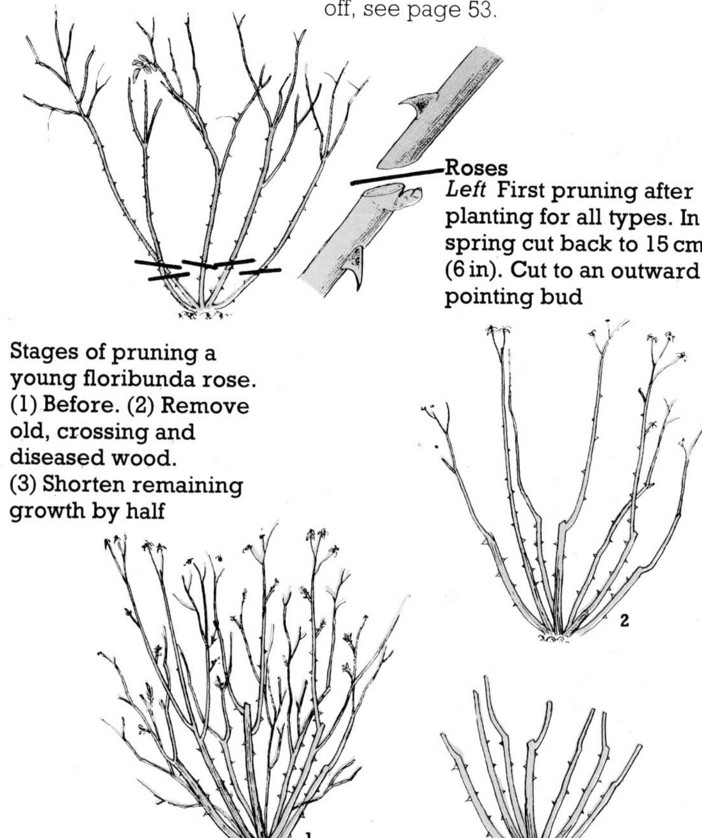

Roses
Left **First pruning after planting for all types. In spring cut back to 15 cm (6 in). Cut to an outward pointing bud**

Stages of pruning a young floribunda rose. (1) Before. (2) Remove old, crossing and diseased wood. (3) Shorten remaining growth by half

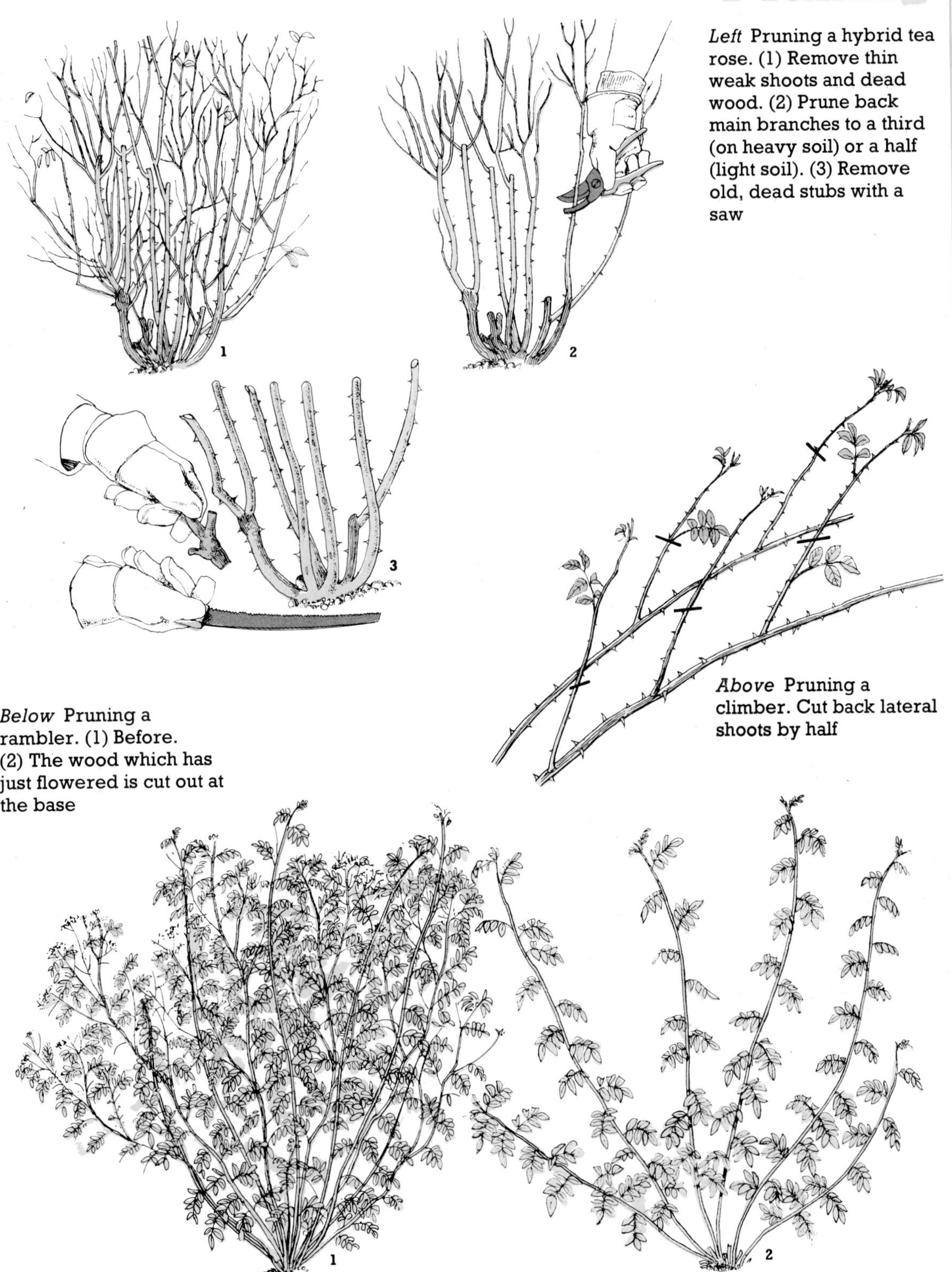

Left Pruning a hybrid tea rose. (1) Remove thin weak shoots and dead wood. (2) Prune back main branches to a third (on heavy soil) or a half (light soil). (3) Remove old, dead stubs with a saw

Above Pruning a climber. Cut back lateral shoots by half

Below Pruning a rambler. (1) Before. (2) The wood which has just flowered is cut out at the base

Types of plants

Described here are the main groups of plants. In this country, three further definitions apply to each group, namely half-hardy, hardy and tender.

Half-hardy plants are those which will not survive much frost and which are grown out of doors only during the summer months.

Hardy plants can stand up to all the normal weather conditions.

Tender plants must be grown under some form of protection throughout the year.

Annuals

These are plants which grow for one year or less during which they germinate from seed, produce their flowers and then die. Hardy annuals are those which can be sown out of doors in early spring for flowering in the summer or, in areas where the winter is not too cold, they can be sown in the autumn and will then come into flower earlier the following year.

Half-hardy annuals are slightly tender plants which will not survive frost and will die if sown outside too early. Ideally these should be sown in boxes in early spring, pricked out and hardened off and planted out after the last frost. Alternatively, sow outdoors in early April, but keep the seedlings and young plants under cloches.

There is no really clear cut division between the plants falling into these two groups, so much depends on the weather or even on the part of the country.

Tender annuals are generally raised and grown on under glass.

Many of the annuals, hardy and half-hardy, are raised in boxes or pots under glass by nurserymen and can be bought as young plants. These

Half-hardy annuals

	Height	Planting distance	Flower colour	Flowering season
Ageratum	13-30 cm (5-12 in)	15-30 cm (6-12 in)	blue	June-September
Callistephus chinensis (aster)	45 cm (18 in)	30 cm (12 in)	white, cream, pinks, red, lilac	July-October
Celosia (cockscomb)	60 cm (24 in)	30 cm (12 in)	red, orange, yellow	July-September
Cosmea (cosmos)	60 cm-1 m (2-3 ft)	60 cm (2 ft)	shades of red and vermilion	August-September
Impatiens balsamina (busy lizzie)	23-75 cm (9 in-2½ ft)	45 cm (1½ ft)	pinks, reds	June-September
Nemesia	20-45 cm (8-18 in)	10-15 cm (4-6 in)	white, yellow, purple	June-August
Nicotiana (tobacco plant)	60 cm-1 m (2-3 ft)	30 cm (1 ft)	white, cream, red, pink, lime green	June-September
Petunia	23-38 cm (9-15 in)	30 cm (1 ft)	pink, white, red, mauve	June-October
Salpiglossis	60 cm (2 ft)	30 cm (1 ft)	crimson, scarlet, orange, yellow, lavender	July-September
Tagetes patula (French marigold)	20-30 cm (8-12 in)	30 cm (1 ft)	yellow, orange	June-October
Zinnia elegans	60-75 cm (2-2½ ft)	30 cm (1 ft)	yellow, pink, red, white	July-September

Hardy annuals

	Height	Planting distance	Flower colour	Flowering season
Alyssum maritimum	8-15 cm (3-6 in)	20-30 cm (8-12 in)	white, pink, purple	June-September
Calendula officinalis (pot marigold)	60 cm (2 ft)	30-38 cm (12-15 in)	orange, yellow	May-October
Clarkia elegans	60 cm (2 ft)	30 cm (1 ft)	white, red, pink, lavender	July-September
Centaurea cyanus (cornflower)	23 cm-1 m (9 in-3 ft)	23-38 cm (9-15 in)	blue, pink	June-September
Convolvulus tricolor	30-38 cm (12-15 in)	15-23 cm (6-9 in)	blue	July-September
Eschscholzia californica (Californian poppy)	30-38 cm (12-15 in)	15 cm (6 in)	orange-yellow	June-October
Godetia grandiflora	30-38 cm (12-15 in)	15 cm (6 in)	rose-purple	June-August
Iberis sempervirens (candytuft)	23 cm (9 in)	30 cm (1 ft)	white	May-June
Malcolmia martima (Virginian stock)	20 cm (8 in)	15 cm (6 in)	red, lilac, rose, white	June-September
Nigella (love-in-a-mist)	60 cm (2 ft)	23 cm (9 in)	blue	June-August
Scabiosa (sweet scabious)	1 m (3 ft)	23 cm (9 in)	crimson	July-September

transplant well, grow away quickly and save you the task of rescuing the seeds from depredations of the birds.

Planting Annuals prefer a sunny position and well-drained light soil. Ease the plants out of the boxes or pots, gently teasing apart the roots if these have become tangled and plant in holes. Firm in well and water thoroughly.

Whether grown from seed sown outside or planted out from boxes or pots, once the plants have established themselves and show signs of making stem growth, give a top-dressing of general fertiliser and pinch out all the tips of the young growth to encourage bushiness.

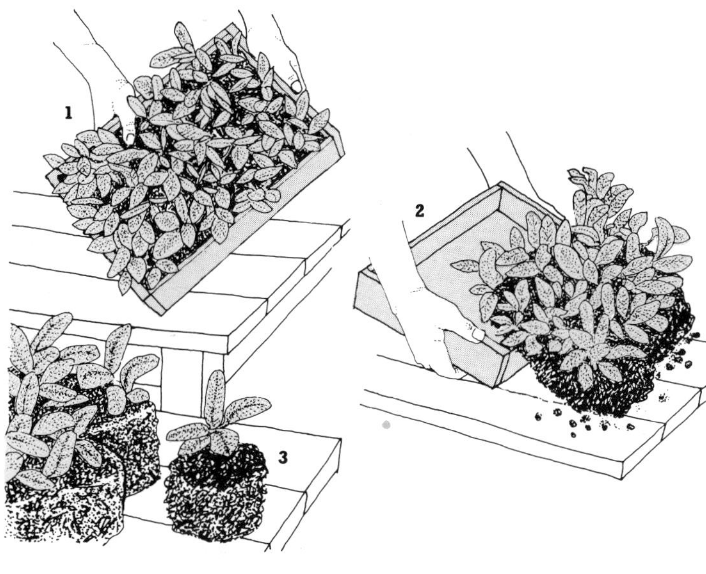

Planting bedding plants. (1) Bang sides of box to loosen the soil. (2) 'Jump' plants out of the box. (3) Separate the plants carefully so that each has a good root. (4) Plant, and firm well

Biennials

	Height	Planting distance	Flower colour	Flowering season
Dianthus barbatus (sweet william)	30-60 cm (1-2 ft)	20-25 cm (8-10 in)	white to red	June-July
Digitalis purpurea (foxglove)	1-1·5 m (3-5 ft)	60 cm (2 ft)	pink, purple, white	June-July
Erysimum alpinum (alpine wallflower)	15 cm (6 in)	10-15 cm (4-6 in)	yellow	May-June
Lunaria annua (honesty)	15-23 cm (6-9 in)	15-23 cm (6-9 in)	violet	June-August
Myosotis (forget-me-not)	8-20 cm (3-8 in)	15 cm (6 in)	blue	April-June
Oenothera (evening primrose)	15-60 cm (6 in-2 ft)	30 cm (1 ft)	yellow	June-August

Above **Removing dead flowers from annuals encourages more buds to form**

Helpful hint

Frequent removal of all dead flower-heads prevents the plants from diverting their energies into producing seed and lengthens the flowering season. When flowering is finished, the plants are pulled up and discarded.

Biennials

These plants take two years to complete their life span, spending their first year from seed in making leafy growth, producing flowers in their second year and then dying.

Dividing herbaceous perennials. (1) By using two forks back to back and levering them apart

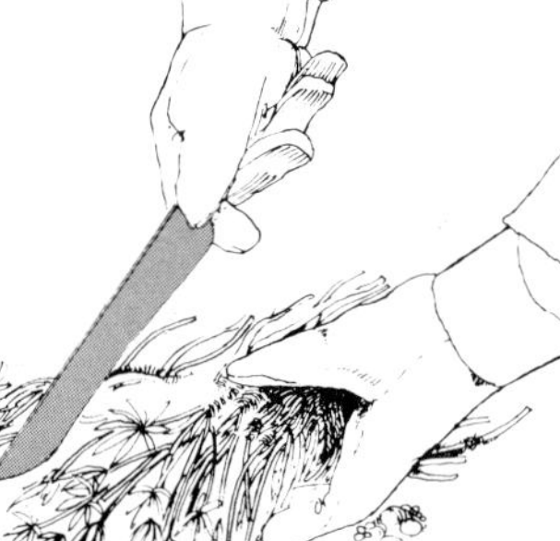

Alternatively, for less strong-growing plants, cut through the root system with a knife (2)

Perennials

Those plants which have a life of several years often, in the case of trees and shrubs, very many years. Herbaceous perennials are distinguished from trees and shrubs (woody perennials) by their soft top growth which in many cases dies down each year to grow afresh in the spring. Some are evergreen and keep their foliage all the year.

Herbaceous perennials can be raised from seeds, in which case they usually take more than one year to reach flowering size; by softwood cuttings of young shoots, again taking two years to reach flowering size; or by division of the clumps in autumn or spring when the plants will usually flower in the first year.

The herbaceous perennials are again divided into hardy, half-hardy and tender. The hardy herbaceous perennials are very versatile and are among the most useful of plants in the garden, requiring a minimum of attention. They benefit from a topdressing of general fertiliser followed by a mulch of organic matter applied in early summer. Many tend to be tall growing and require some form of support – always rather unsightly until the plants grow up sufficiently to hide it – and life is easier if you choose those which don't need staking, for example, dictamnus, geum, mon-

Hardy perennials

	Height	Planting distance	Flower colour	Flowering period
Achillea filipendulina (yarrow)	1-1·25 m (3-4 ft)	1-1·25 m (3-4 ft)	yellow	July-Sept
Anemone japonica (Japanese anemone)	60 cm-1 m (2-3 ft)	30-45 cm (1-1½ ft)	pink, white	August-October
Aster novi-belgii (Michaelmas daisy)	75 cm-1·25 m (2½-4 ft)	38 cm (15 in)	pink, blue, purple, crimson	Sept-October
Campanula (bellflower)	30 cm-1·25 m (1-4 ft)	15-60 cm (6 in-2 ft)	blue, white	July, August
Convallaria majalis (lily of the valley)	18 cm (7 in)	60 cm (2 ft)	white, bell-like flowers sweetly scented	April-May
Delphinium varieties	1-1·5 m (3-5 ft)	45-60 cm (1½-2 ft)	blue, cream, lilac	June-August
Euphorbia varieties (spurge)	30-60 cm (1-2 ft)	60 cm (2 ft)	sulphur yellow, red	March-July
Helianthus decapetalus (perennial sunflower)	1·25-2 m (4-6 ft)	45-60 cm (1½-2 ft)	yellow	July-September
Kniphofia varieties (red hot poker)	60 cm-1·5 m (2-5 ft)	60 cm (2 ft)	flame, orange, yellow	June-October
Paeonia lactiflora varieties (peony)	60 cm (2 ft)	1 m (3 ft)	crimson to white	May-June
Pyrethrum roseum varieties	1 m (3 ft)	45 cm (1½ ft)	white to red	May-June
Solidago (golden rod)	1-2 m (3-6 ft)	75 cm (2½ ft)	yellow	August-October

arda, montbretia, physostegia, rudbeckia, the sedums and tradescantia.

In the autumn, the plants can be tidied up, dead foliage and flower stems removed and, except for the evergreen plants, the growth can be cut off to a couple of inches above soil level.

Most perennials eventually grow into large clumps and become less vigorous; every few years these clumps should be divided, the centre being discarded and the younger shoots around the edges replanted. Do this in early spring or autumn.

Trees and shrubs

These groups of plants, in fact, they are woody perennials, are not only hardy, half-hardy or tender but, and more important for us, evergreen or deciduous. The evergreen trees and shrubs are those which retain their leaves throughout the winter, while the deciduous drop their leaves in the autumn.

When choosing a tree for the garden, bear in mind its ultimate height and how fast it grows. There is no place in the small garden for a forest tree such as the ash, elm, beech, oak or lime. They get too big and have to be pollarded. This is a method of cutting back which disfigures the trees and leaves them standing like scarecrows. Tall trees cast shadows, block out light and may even undermine house foundations.

Flowering trees such as the Japanese flowering cherries, the crab apples and laburnums are always good value, also the lovely golden *Robinia* Frisia and the smaller weeping trees such as the weeping pear (*Pyrus salicifolius pendulus*), weeping cherry (*Prunus subhirtella* Pendula

Types of plants

Trees

	Height	Spread	Description
Acer ginnala	6 m (20 ft)	3 m (10 ft)	spreading habit, rich autumn colour
Betula pendula (silver birch)	6-9 m (20-30 ft)	2·5-3·5 m (8-12 ft)	weeping habit, silver bark, light canopy
Crataegus monogyna (hawthorn)	7·5-9 m (25-30 ft)	4·5-6 m (15-20 ft)	white flowers in May, red berries in autumn
Chamaecyparis lawsoniana (Lawson's cypress)	50 m (160 ft)	4·5 m (15 ft)	grows rapidly, used as hedging
Laburnum anagyroides	3-6 m (10-20 ft)	2·5-3·5 m (8-12 ft)	yellow flowers in spring, light canopy
Liriodendron tulipifera (tulip tree)	6-7·5 m (20-25 ft)	3-4·5 m (10-15 ft)	light green leaves turn to yellow in autumn
Malus (crab apple)	3-6 m (10-20 ft)	3-6 m (10-20 ft)	flowers in spring, attractive fruit later in the year
Prunus (flowering cherry)	4·5-12 m (15-40 ft)	4·5-9 m (15-30 ft)	attractive bark, lovely show of pink or white blossom in spring
Pyrus salicifolia (weeping pear)	4·5-6·5 m (15-25 ft)	3-6 m (10-20 ft)	silver foliage, weeping habit
Robinia pseudoacacia 'Frisia' (false acacia)	6-9 m (20-30 ft)	3-4·5 m (10-15 ft)	golden yellow foliage
Sorbus aucuparia (mountain ash)	4·5-6·5 m (15-25 ft)	2·5-4 m (8-12 ft)	white flowers in May, red berries in autumn
Thuja occidentalis	7·5 m (25 ft)	4·5 m (15 ft)	bronze-green foliage

Rosea), weeping cotoneaster (*Cotoneaster* Hybridus Pendulus) and weeping birch (*Betula pendula* Youngii). For the larger garden silver birches are a good choice with their coloured bark and dainty habit of growth.

Useful as a tree can be to create a focal point or to provide a shady spot, it is the shrubs which form the backbone of the garden, providing the basic outline for any planting scheme and mixing especially well with herbaceous perennials, roses and bulbs.

The choice is wide depending only on where you wish to put the emphasis – flowers, fruits or foliage. I always think it is important to consider especially the value of evergreens. They furnish the garden at a time when other trees and shrubs are leafless, and provide shelter for other plants and for ourselves. Those with coloured or variegated foliage like *Elaeagnus pungens maculatus* and the variegated hollies bring colour into the garden and light up in the winter sunshine, and the silvers and greys provide a total contrast and year-round interest.

Roses

These are probably still the most versatile and popular of all garden plants. When grown in beds, as

When planting trees, their different habits must be considered and a suitable one chosen. A range of tree shapes is shown below.
(1) Japanese maple, *Acer palmatum dissectum*.
(2) Weeping Birch, *Betula pendula Youngii*.
(3) Hawthorn, Crataegus.
(4) Japanese cherry, *Prunus* Amanogawa.
(5) Laburnum

1

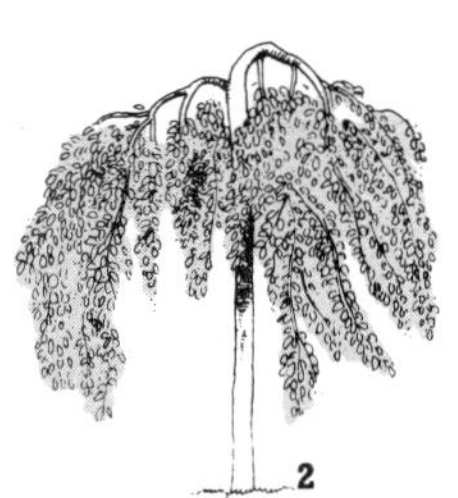
2

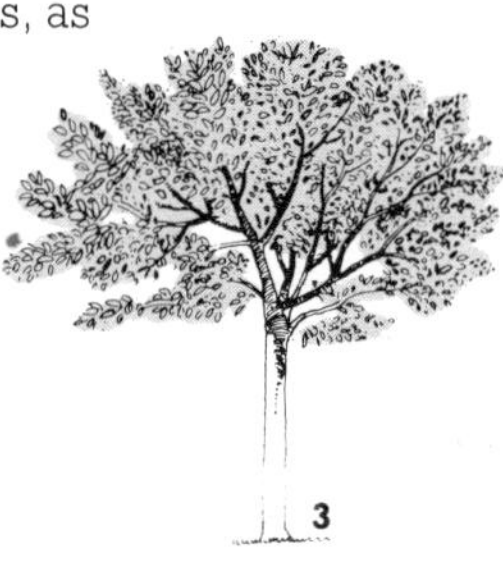
3

4

Above **The best way of removing rose suckers is to trace them back to the point of origin and pull them off**

specimen shrubs, as hedges or as climbers, the rose has a lot to offer, but the choice is immense and can be just a little bewildering. We have the plant breeders to thank for this, working over many years they have produced a variety of types, the main kinds of which are as follows:

Hybrid teas These have large, shapely, and often fragrant blooms produced more or less continuously from June to October. They are especially good for cutting.

Floribundas Flowering over the same period as the hybrid teas but more abundantly, and the single or semi-double flowers are carried in clusters. The taller varieties make good hedges. Growth habit similar to the hybrid teas.

Ramblers and other climbers
Ramblers are vigorous climbers which bear small flowers in large clusters; as a rule they flower only once during the year.

The most useful group of climbers are, without doubt, the repeat-flowering climbers with a less rampant growth habit which bloom throughout the summer.

There are also the climbing sports of the floribundas and hybrid teas which have a shorter flowering season but are capable of growing very tall (up to 6 m, 20 ft).

Miniature Growing to about 45 cm (18 in) high, these dainty roses look like small floribundas and are useful for edging rose beds or growing in containers. Free flowering.

Shrub roses A category used to describe most of the other roses. Generally they are vigorous and bush like and carry clusters of single, semi-double or fully double flowers, in some cases throughout a long season. They need very little pruning and make good ornamental hedges or specimen shrubs.

Included here are the old-fashioned roses, the modern shrub and the hybrids derived from the wild and other species of roses.

The site Roses do best in an open, sunny position but with shelter from north and east winds. Good drainage is important and the soil should be well cultivated and have some organic matter dug in to it.

Planting This can take place any time between mid-October and the end of March but the soil must be in a workable condition and free from frost. Plant as described on page 41. Container-grown plants can be put in at any time of the year.

Aftercare I like to feed roses in spring and again during the summer using a rose fertiliser and applying this at the rate of 110 g to the sq m (4 oz to the sq yd). A mulch of organic matter applied in early summer can do nothing but good, as it protects the soil from losing too much moisture and keeps down weeds.

Look out for suckers; these are shoots which grow from the root system and weaken the plants if not attended to. They always differ in appearance from the rest of the growth generally having small pale green leaves and a lot of thorns. Do not cut them as this only increases the problem, instead remove the soil, trace them back to their point of origin and pull them out.

Early in the year I keep a look out for signs of greenfly and mildew – both of which are difficult to eradicate if they get a hold. Spray at the earliest sign with a systemic fungicide mixed with a systemic insecticide.

During the flowering period it is worth taking the trouble to remove fading blooms from the hybrid teas. This encourages new flowers to open and prevents the formation of hips.

Pruning This is dealt with on pages 44-47.

Hedges

I always think that a hedge makes a much more natural background to the garden than a fence or wall; it provides shelter and is cheaper than any form of fencing as well as requiring, on the whole, a minimum amount of maintenance.

As a windbreak, a hedge is more effective than a wall as it allows the wind to filter through and reduces its velocity. Wind hitting a wall, on the other hand, bounces over the top and creates eddies inside to the detriment of the plants growing there.

Tall or low growing, clipped or informal, there is a hedging plant for every purpose. One thing they have in common is the fact that they are intended to be a permanent feature in the garden and therefore should be chosen with care and planted in well-prepared soil.

Preparing the soil

1 Dig the soil thoroughly, forking in some organic matter and adding a dressing of a slow-acting fertiliser such as bonemeal at 110 gm to the sq m (4 oz to the sq yd).

2 Sprinkle a dressing of hydrated lime 110 gm to the sq m (4 oz to the sq yd) over the surface if the soil is acid.

3 Allow about one month for the soil to settle.

Planting the hedge

The planting times are the same as for other shrubs, see page 40. There are two methods of planting: either take out a trench 38 to 45 cm (15 to 18 in) wide and the length of the intended hedge, or dig individual planting holes. The latter method is mainly used for shrubs planted 60 cm (2 ft) or more apart.

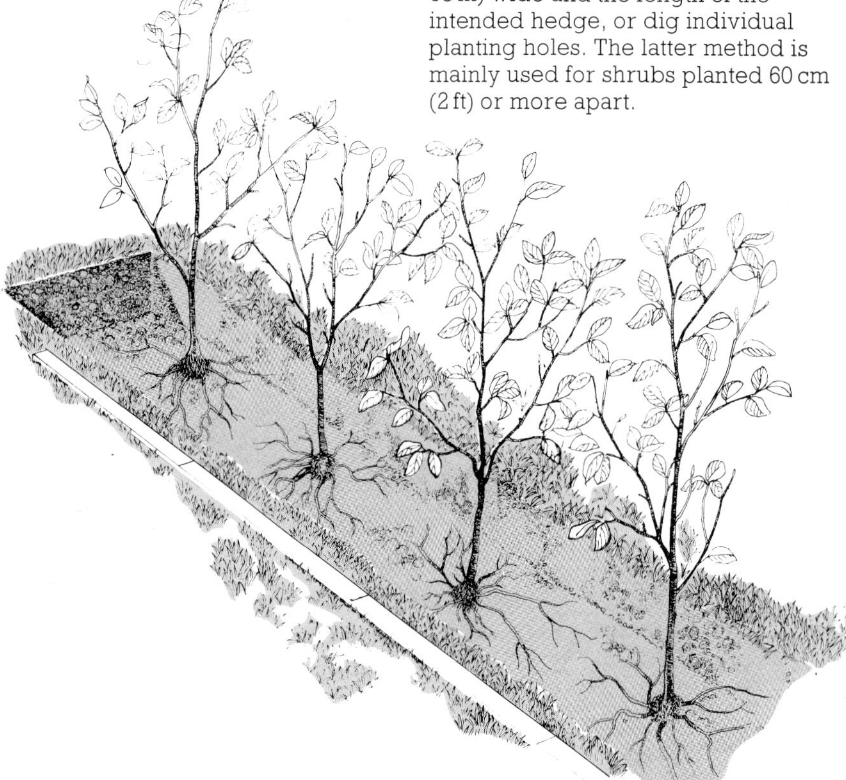

Planting a row of hedging plants in a trench. Spread the roots well (*left*), then return the soil and firm each plant (*above*)

The planting of various kinds of shrubs has already been described on page 40. It is important to plant firmly, spacing at the recommended distances and keeping the shrubs to the depth they were originally growing at. It may be necessary to provide the support of canes or horizontally trained wires in the early stages.

Give an annual feed with a general fertiliser in spring and mulch with organic matter.

The choice of plants

The majority of shrubs can be used for hedges or screens, I have given here some of my own favourites.

Formal hedges are those which are kept clipped regularly. Informal hedges show the natural shape of the shrub and are trimmed occasionally with secateurs to remove long or straggly growths. Do not trim flowering and berrying hedges too hard or they will produce only a few flowers and berries.

Berberis darwinii 2 to 2·5 m (6 to 8 ft). Evergreen, deep yellow flowers in spring followed by plum-coloured berries in autumn. Trim after flowers fade if informal, or clip in late summer. Plant 45 to 60 cm (18 to 24 in) apart.

Berberis thunbergii atropurpurea 1 to 1·25 m (3 to 4 ft). Young shoots coral pink backed by dark bronze leaves, red and yellow flowers, red berries. Trim in March. Plant 38 to 45 cm (15 to 18 in) apart.

Carpinus betulus (Hornbeam) 3 to 6 m (10 to 20 ft). Deciduous, similar to beech – the brown leaves remain on the hedge all winter. Do not prune for the first two years then trim in late summer. Allow to reach the required height before taking the top out. Plant 45 cm (18 in) apart.

Chamaecyparis lawsoniana (Lawson Cypress). Conifer from 1 to 7·5 m (3 to 25 ft) depending on the variety. Green Hedger grows to a height of 4·5 m (15 ft) and is especially recommended.

Trim in late summer, cut hard back if necessary in spring. Allow to reach the required height before taking the top out. Plant 45 to 60 cm (18 to 24 in) apart.

Cotoneaster 2 to 3 m (6 to 10 ft). Several species both evergreen and deciduous. The white flowers are followed by red berries in autumn. Clip or trim in late winter. Plant 45 cm (18 in) apart.

Until it becomes established, a young hedge may well need some form of support. Here the plants are tied to a horizontal wire stretched between posts

Hedges

Crataegus monogyna (Hawthorn, May) 2 to 4·5 m (6 to 15 ft). White flowers followed by red berries. Trim any time between October and March. Plant 30 cm (12 in) apart.

Cupressocyparis leylandii (Leyland Cypress) 3 m (10 ft). Dark green conifer with good golden form called Castlewellan. Fastest growing of all hedges. Allow to grow to required height before taking the top out, tip the branches back in summer. Plant 60 to 90 cm (24 to 36 in) apart.

Escallonia 2 to 2·5 m (6 to 8 ft). Evergreen shrubs, suitable for seaside gardens. A number of good varieties with shiny foliage and pink or red flowers. Clip after the flowers fade. Plant 30 to 45 cm (12 to 18 in) apart.

Euonymus japonicus 2·5 to 3·5 m (8 to 12 ft). Evergreen shrub suitable for seaside gardens. Trim occasionally during the summer. Plant 45 cm (18 in) apart.

Fagus (Beech) 3 m (10 ft). Deciduous, but the brown leaves are retained during the winter. Do not clip for the first two years then clip in summer; allow to reach the required height before taking out the top. Plant 45 cm (18 in) apart.

Ilex (Holly) Up to 6 m (20 ft). Evergreen but with golden and silver variegated forms. Very slow growing. Trim in late summer, cut hard back if necessary in early spring. Plant 30 to 45 cm (12 to 18 in) apart.

Lavandula (Lavender) 1·25 m (4 ft). Good informal ever-grey hedge with scented foliage. Trim in spring. Plant 45 cm (18 in) apart.

Ligustrum (Privet) 1·2 to 2·5 m (4 to 8 ft). Evergreen or semi-evergreen with golden and green forms. Clip at least twice a year. Plant 30 to 45 cm (12 to 18 in) apart.

Lonicera nitida (Honeysuckle) 1·25 m (4 ft). Neat evergreen foliage. Trim several times in summer. Plant 30 cm (12 in) apart.

Pyracantha (Firethorn) 2 m (6 ft). Evergreen with white flowers in late spring and red, yellow or orange berries in autumn. Several species available. Trim in spring if grown as an informal hedge. Clipped hedges will not carry many berries. Plant 45 to 60 cm (18 to 24 in) apart.

Ribes (Flowering Currant) 2·5 m (8 ft). Deciduous, red flowers in spring. Trim after flowering. Plant 45 cm (18 in) apart.

Rosmarinus officinalis (Rosemary) 1 m (3 ft). Evergreen, aromatic shiny foliage, blue flowers in spring. Trim after flowering. Plant 30 to 38 cm (12 to 15 in) apart.

Rosa (Rose) 2 m (7 ft). Look for the *rugosa* varieties with their decorative flowers followed by large hips. Remove old flowers and trim back slightly at the same time. Never plant *canina* or *laxa*. Plant 60 cm to 1 m (2 to 3 ft) apart.

Santolina incana (Lavender Cotton) 60 cm (2 ft). Evergreen with silvery foliage and yellow flowers in summer. Trim off dead flowers, clip in spring. Plant 30 cm (12 in) apart.

Thuya plicata 3·5 m (12 ft). Dark green conifer with a golden form *T.p. zebrina*. Allow plants to reach the required height before taking out the tops. Trim in late summer.

Pruning hedges. Ligustrum, crataegus. (1) 1st year – cut down to 15 cm (6 in) from the ground. (2) 2nd year – cut away half the new growth. (3) 3rd year – trim the sides short and allow the top to grow taller

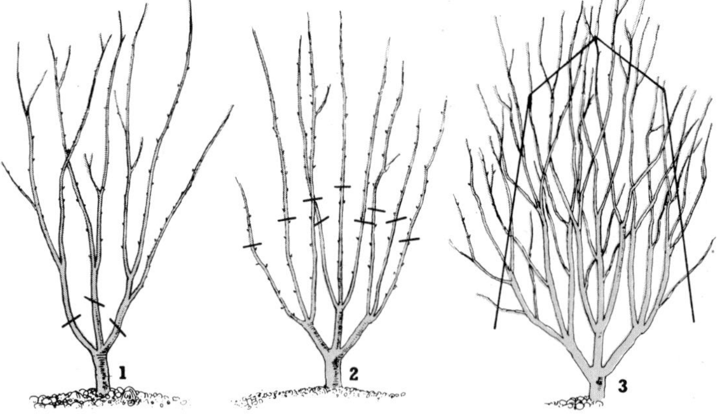

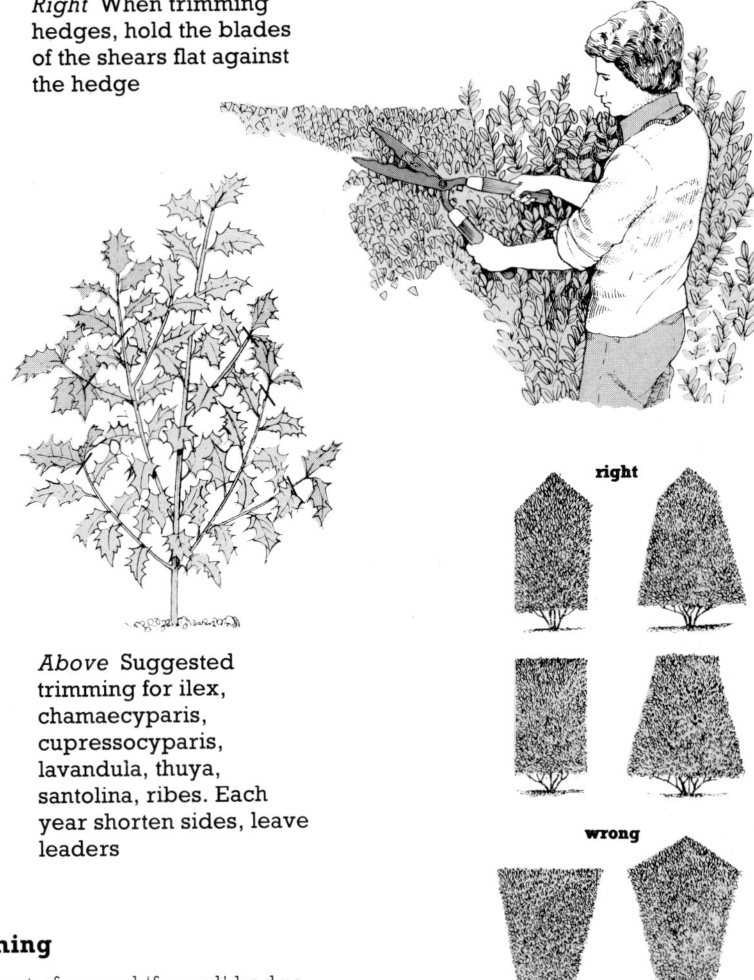

Right When trimming hedges, hold the blades of the shears flat against the hedge

Above Suggested trimming for ilex, chamaecyparis, cupressocyparis, lavandula, thuya, santolina, ribes. Each year shorten sides, leave leaders

Hedge tops may be cut on a slant in snowy areas. Never cut the bottom narrower than the top

Suggested trimming for cotoneaster, escallonia, euonymus, fagus, lonicera, pyracantha, rosmarinus, rosa. *Top* After planting shorten side shoots. *Above* 2nd winter – shorten side shoots. Subsequently, shorten side growth and allow hedge to grow taller

Trimming

The secret of a good 'formal' hedge is regular trimming and a battery, electric or motor-powered trimmer makes the job a whole lot easier. However, the number of trimmings required varies with the type of hedge: privet may need 4 or 5 trims a year but I find *Cupressocyparis leylandii* only requires cutting twice a year, and *Chamaecyparis lawsoniana*, thuya, beech and hornbeam only need one cut a year in August or early September.

Broad-leaved evergreens are better pruned with secateurs rather than a powered trimmer or shears which cut indiscriminately through the foliage and spoil its appearance.

Helpful hint

In areas where heavy snowfalls are a common winter occurrence, it is better to cut the hedge with a sloping rather than a flat top – make a point and bring the sides down at an angle of about 45 degrees before allowing them to fall straight down.

Ground cover and climbing plants

Plants for ground cover

Ground cover is the term used to describe a range of creeping or trailing plants which have all the advantages of forming a carpet-like, weed-smothering covering to the soil while requiring very little maintenance. They can be used as an alternative to grass in areas of low traffic or as a very decorative garden feature in their own right.

One of my favourite plants for this purpose is the heath *Erica carnea* and its two best varieties Springwood Pink and Springwood White. These keep flat, spreading themselves over the ground rooting as they go, and provide flowers from November to March.

There are other varieties which offer flowers throughout the twelve months of the year as well as, in some cases, bright coloured foliage, and all of these will tolerate lime. Choose from the following: *Erica carnea* Aurea, *E.c.* Winter Beauty, *E.*x *darleyensis*, *E.*x *darleyensis* Silberschmeize (Silver Beads), *E. vagans* Lyonesse, *E.v.* Mrs D.F. Maxwell, *Calluna vulgaris* H.E. Beale.

Next in value to the ericas I would put St John's Wort or the Rose of Sharon (*Hypericum calycinum*). This spreads by underground roots and is good under trees and in dense shade. Put the shears over it in March each year or knock the tops off with a scythe and plenty of young shoots will come up from below to give large, yellow poppy-like flowers throughout the summer.

On banks in dense shade ivy or one of its variegated forms makes exceptionally good ground cover. I have even seen ivy establish itself under yew trees and this must surely be one of the most difficult areas.

If you can use ground cover plants with flowers or berries so much the better, and variegated foliage must always be considered as a bonus for the added interest it will bring.

Planting

Where you are planting ground cover plants in areas under trees and shrubs, you must give them good care in the initial stages to get them established, otherwise the competition with the roots of the shrubs and trees for moisture and plant food will prove too much for them. When planting, prepare a good size hole, put in some peat and fresh soil and plant into this. Keep them well watered during the first few months. Once established they will look after themselves.

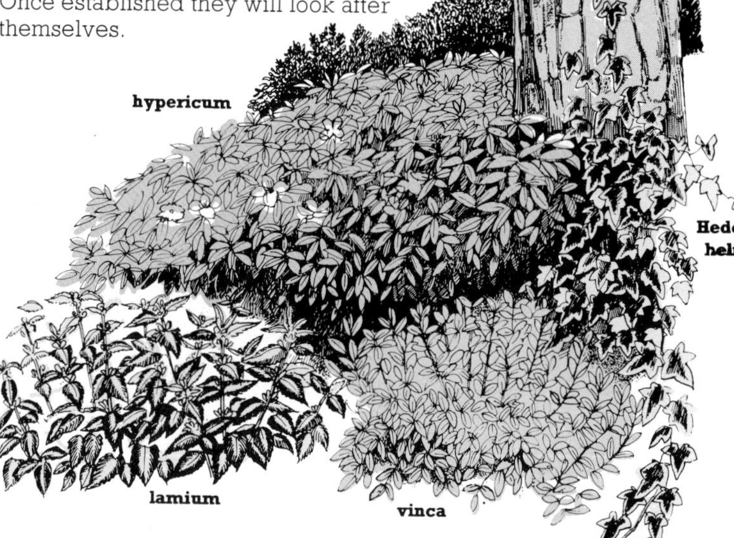

A ground cover planting scheme. Ensure that the plants get off to a good start by planting them in a mixture of peat and fresh soil

A further selection of ground cover plants

Ajuga reptans Range of varieties with coloured and variegated foliage in purple, bronze, red or cream. Blue flowers in early summer. Good in sun or semi-shade.

Bergenia (Elephant's Ears) Bold foliage and clusters of handsome pink flowers in late winter and early spring. Good choice for shrub borders.

Cotoneaster The prostrate species, such as *C. adpressus praecox*, *C.*

dammeri and *C. horizontalis*, keep flat and root as they go. Berry bearing.

Juniper Prostrate forms *Juniperus horizontalis* and *J. sabina tamariscifolia* are exceptionally good on banks. They need an open position and will grow on chalk.

Lamium (Dead Nettle) Yellow, silvery and green foliage. One variety, Silver Beacon, is particularly fine in colour. Sunny or shady position.

Lysimachia nummularia (Creeping Jenny) Green or gold foliage with yellow flowers in spring. For moist shade.

Pachysandra terminalis Good evergreen cover, there is one form with variegated leaves. Will not stand as much shade as ivy or hypericum.

Roses The very vigorous climbing roses make excellent ground cover for banks, just plant and allow them to trail. Try also the prostrate growing Max Graf (a *rugosa* hybrid).

Stachys lanata (Lamb's Ears) Roots as it goes. The grey woolly foliage is very appealing and I like to use it between roses and to form an edging. Needs a sunny, well-drained position. The variety Silver Carpet is non-flowering.

Vinca minor and V. major (Periwinkle) Green and variegated forms with blue or white flowers in spring. Will stand dense shade, can be grown under north-facing walls, between other shrubs and on top of dry walls and banks. They root as they go and will cover large areas.

Helpful hint

If using ground cover between roses, then the roses will want extra feed in the early part of the year and also in summer.

Climbing plants

The importance of climbing plants in a garden should never be underestimated. They are a means of clothing walls, disguising garages and garden buildings, making decorative screens and, most important of all in the small garden, they make the area larger by allowing you to garden upwards.

The plants used for this purpose may be true climbers, which by means of aerial roots (ivy), sucker pads (Virginia creeper), tendrils or twining stems (honeysuckle) cling of their accord to walls or other forms of support, or they may be shrubs which are not true climbers and need to be trained in and tied to a support. Plastic-covered netting, a wooden trellis or wires stretched between special vine eyes knocked into the masonry provide support for all wall plants. Try to mount these at least 8 cm (3 in) away from the wall to allow for air circulation behind the plants as this helps to prevent attacks of mildew and other diseases and pests.

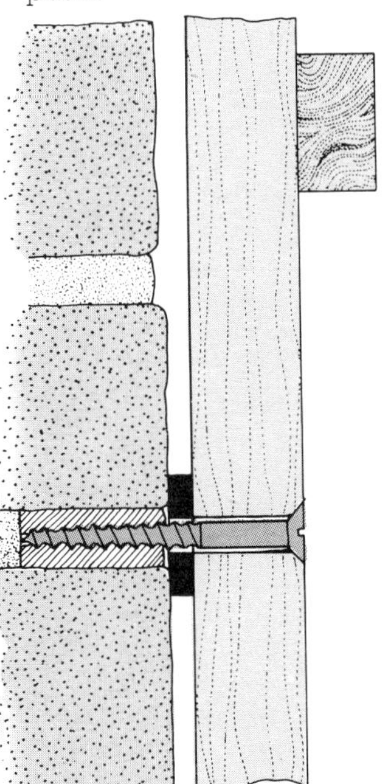

Wooden trellises can be attached to a wall by screws. Place a rubber washer over the screw to hold the trellis away from the wall

Ground cover and climbing plants

Planting

Climbers are planted in the same way as other shrubs, the holes being dug at least 30 cm (12 in) away from the base of a wall or fence so that the plant is inclined backwards at a slight angle. This allows more water to reach the roots and keeps the plants out of the very dry areas which occur at the bottom of walls and fences. Clematis always appreciate a cool root run, although their heads should be in the sun, so try to arrange for the roots to be shaded by a low-growing shrub or large flat pebbles.

Aftercare

Watch the watering as it is all too easy for climbers to suffer from the effects of dry or freely draining soil. Topdress once a year or so with general garden fertiliser and apply a mulch of organic matter in early summer to help cut down the evaporation of soil moisture.

Plant climbers at least 30 cm (12 in) away from the wall where the soil will not be so dry

Pruning has already been mentioned (see page 46) but I would like to point out that the true climbers are easily spoiled by overpruning. Those that flower in the early part of the year are trimmed back after the last of the blooms have died, and summer flowerers are pruned in late winter.

Choosing climbers and wall shrubs

The important point to bear in mind in choosing wall plants is the aspect of the wall, fence or screen: north-facing ones mean that the plants will get little sunshine, south-facing that there may be an excess of sun and warmth, while east facing are often subjected to cold winds.

Climbers and wall shrubs

	Height	Aspect	Features	Flowers	Mode of attachment
Actinidia kolomikta	6 m (20 ft)	S/W	deciduous, slender, leaves partly pink	white flowers in June	twining
Ceanothus (Californian lilacs)	up to 3·5 m (12 ft)	S/W	deciduous or evergreen, needs good drainage	blue, white or mauve flowers in spring, summer or autumn	requires training
Chaenomeles (japonica, quince)	up to 2·5 m (8 ft)	any	deciduous, easily cultivated	red, pink, orange or white flowers in spring followed by yellow quinces	requires training
Clematis species	up to 9 m (30 ft)	depends on species	deciduous and evergreen, roots should be in cool, moist well-drained soil	yellow, white, pink or purple flowers in summer, a few flower in winter; some have attractive seedheads	twining
Garrya elliptica	3 m (10 ft)	any	evergreen, requires protection in cold areas	male plant is draped with long, grey green catkins in winter	requires training
Hedera helix varieties (ivy)	up to 15 m (50 ft)	any	evergreen, withstand atmospheric pollution, and any soil, variegated forms	inconspicuous flowers followed by bunches of fruits	self clinging
Jasminum officinale	6-9 m (20-30 ft)	any	deciduous, delicate foliage	white fragrant flowers from June to September	twining

Climbers and wall shrubs

	Height	Aspect	Features	Flowers	Mode of attachment
J. nudiflorum (winter jasmine)	4·5 m (15 ft)	any	deciduous, green stems in winter	bright yellow flowers from November to February	requires training
Kerria japonica 'Pleniflora'	2 m (6 ft)	any	deciduous, arching green stems in winter	yellow, ball like flowers in April and May	requires training
Lonicera species (honeysuckle)	up to 9 m (30 ft)	S/W	deciduous and evergreen	yellow, cream or pink flowers, often fragrant, from May to December, depending on species, followed by berries	twining
Parthenocissus (Virginia creeper and Boston ivy)	up to 9 m (30 ft)	any	deciduous, leaves turn brilliant orange and scarlet in autumn	inconspicuous flowers, sometimes followed by attractive fruit	self clinging
Passiflora (passion flower)	3 m (10 ft)	S	deciduous, needs sheltered position	spectacular flowers, summer and autumn; in hot years followed by oval, orange edible fruit	twining
Polygonum baldschuanicum (Russian vine)	up to 12 m (40 ft)	S/W	deciduous, rampant	pink flushed flowers from July to October	twining
Pyracantha (firethorn)	up to 5 m (16 ft)	S/E/W	evergreen, glossy leaves, thorny	small pink or white flowers in May and June; red, orange or yellow berries in autumn and winter	requires training
Roses, Zéphirine Drouhin	3 m (10 ft)	any	absence of thorns from main stem, young foliage has a bronze hue	bright carmine, semi-double, strongly scented blooms throughout summer	requires training
Golden Showers	2-3 m (6-10 ft)	any	best in a sheltered position	large, double yellow blooms in clusters, fragrant; very free flowering	requires training
Autumn Sunlight	2·5 m (8 ft)	any	bright green glossy foliage	brilliant orange scented blooms produced throughout summer	requires training
Vitis 'Brandt'	9 m (30 ft)	S	deciduous, attractively shaped foliage, leaves turn purple with pale green veins	bunches of black, sweet, aromatic grapes after a hot dry summer	twining
Wisteria	up to 18 m (60 ft)	S	deciduous, attractive leaves	long clusters of blue, mauve, pink or white flowers in May, June and July, often fragrant	requires training

Bulbs, corms, tubers and rhizomes

All these plants have one thing in common – they store their food in swollen underground parts. Strictly speaking they are all herbaceous perennials, and it is the underground storage organ which remains dormant during the winter and then uses its food supply to produce roots, leaves and flowers when the weather conditions are conducive to growth.

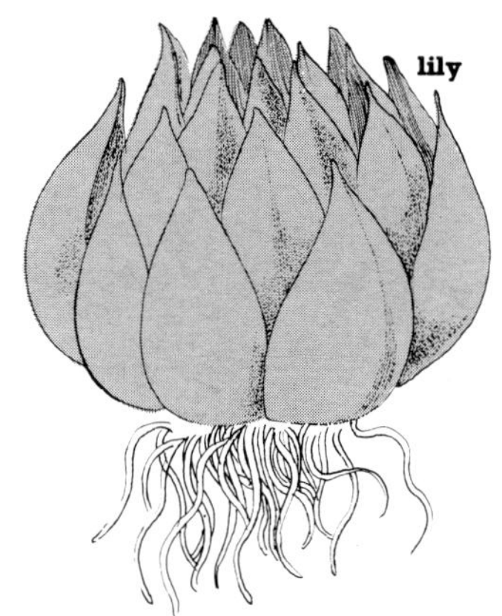

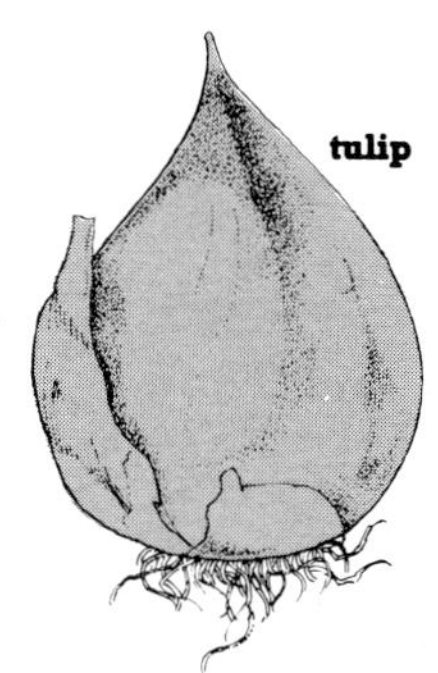

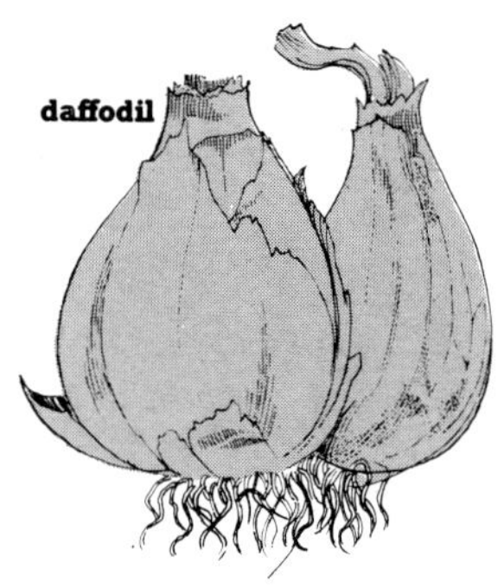

Bulbs Although the term 'bulb' is often rather loosely used to cover this entire group of plants, the true bulb can be distinguished by the layers of swollen leaf bases or scales which surround the new undeveloped shoot. Onions, tulips, daffodils and lilies are examples of bulbs.

Bulbs

	Height	**Planting distance**	**Flower colour**	**Flowering period**
Allium moly	30 cm (1 ft)	10 cm (4 in)	yellow	June-July
Anemone blanda	15 cm (6 in)	10 cm (4 in)	blue	February-April
Colchicum speciosum	15 cm (6 in)	23-30 cm (9-12 in)	mauve	September-November
Crocus vernus	8-13 cm (3-5 in)	8 cm (3 in)	purple	March
Eranthis hyemalis (winter aconite)	10 cm (4 in)	8 cm (3 in)	yellow	February-March
Galanthus nivalis (snowdrop)	8-20 cm (3-8 in)	8-15 cm (3-6 in)	white	January-February
Gladiolus hybrids	60 cm-1·25 m (2-4 ft)	15 cm (6 in)	all colours	July-September
Iris reticulata	15 cm (6 in)	5-10 cm (2-4 in)	deep purple	February-March
Leucojum vernum (snowflake)	20 cm (8 in)	8-10 cm (3-4 in)	white	February-March
Muscari armeniacum	20-25 cm (8-10 in)	8-10 cm (3-4 in)	blue	February-March
Narcissus (daffodil)	15-45 cm (6-18 in)	5-15 cm (2-6 in)	yellow	February-April
Nerine bowdenii	60 cm (2 ft)	15 cm (6 in)	pink	September-November
Tulip	15-60 cm (6 in-2 ft)	15 cm (6 in)	pinks, reds, yellows	April-May

Corms These are completely different, being solid structures, in fact, swollen stems, which carry their buds on the outer surface e.g. crocus, gladiolus.

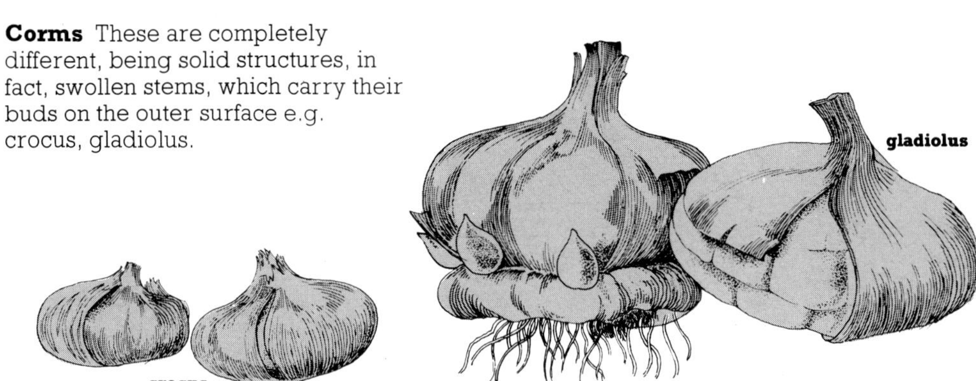

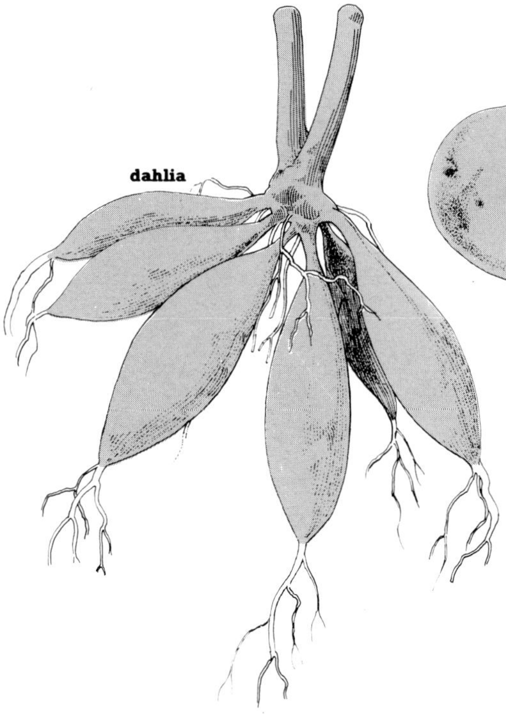

dahlia

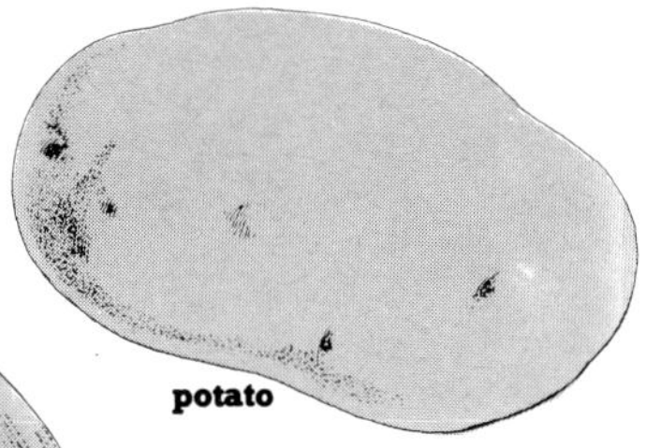

potato

Tubers These are either swollen underground stems with buds or 'eyes' which produce the growth on the surface (a potato is a typical example), or thickened tuberous roots which do not carry a bud and will only sprout if part of the original stem and a bud is left attached (dahlia).

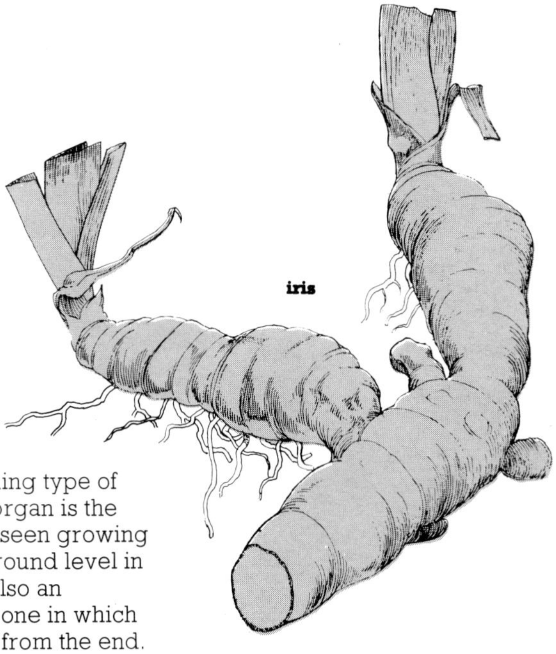

iris

Rhizomes The remaining type of underground storage organ is the rhizome, which can be seen growing at, or slightly below, ground level in beds or irises. This is also an underground stem but one in which the new growth comes from the end.

Bulbs, corms, tubers and rhizomes

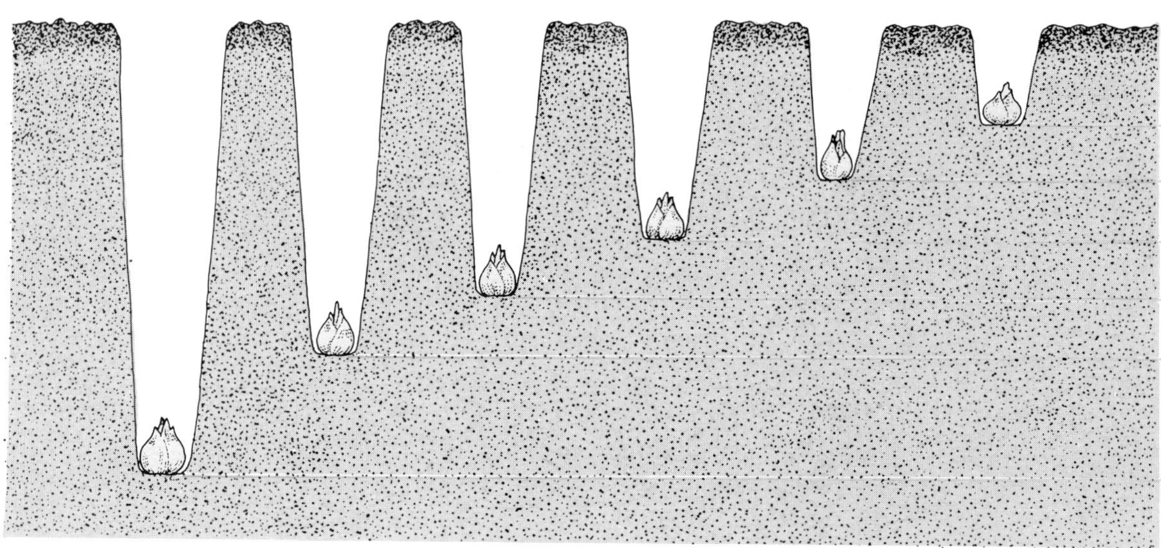

Above Suggested planting depths for a range of bulbs

Soils and planting

'Bulbs' do best in light, freely draining soils. Heavy soils which become waterlogged are not recommended – dig in organic matter to improve the soil structure first, but do not allow bulbs to come into contact with fresh manure.

Plant spring-flowering kinds in autumn, summer-flowering ones in spring. All bulbs benefit from a sprinkling of bonemeal worked into the soil around the planting hole. Put a layer of sand in the bottom of the hole and plant with a trowel to the depth shown in the diagram, as a general rule the bulb should be covered with twice its own depth of soil. Group the bulbs in casual clusters, do not plant in straight lines.

Certain bulbs, for example the daffodils, crocus and anemones, look particularly effective if naturalised in grass: toss a handful on the grass and plant them where they fall.

I have done this in my own garden, planting daffodil Golden Harvest under forsythia bushes, but they look equally good under apples and for another effect try muscari under cherry trees.

Helpful hint

A special tool called a bulb planter is useful for this task as it removes plugs of soil and grass rather in the manner of an apple corer. The bulb is then placed in the hole and the plug of soil replaced and pressed down gently with the foot.

After flowering, the dead flowers and stems are removed but the leaves must be left and allowed to die back naturally. In this way they continue to manufacture food which is then stored underground for the following season. If planted in grass then the grass must not be cut until the bulb leaves have withered.

Once planted most bulbs can be left undisturbed for years, gladiolus corms, however, are an exception. These should be lifted with a fork some six weeks after flowering and the tops cut back. Allow the corms to dry off and store them in shallow boxes in a cool airy place.

Bulbs in pots and bowls

We always like to have some bowls and pots of bulbs, especially hyacinths and daffodils, to brighten

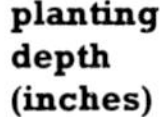

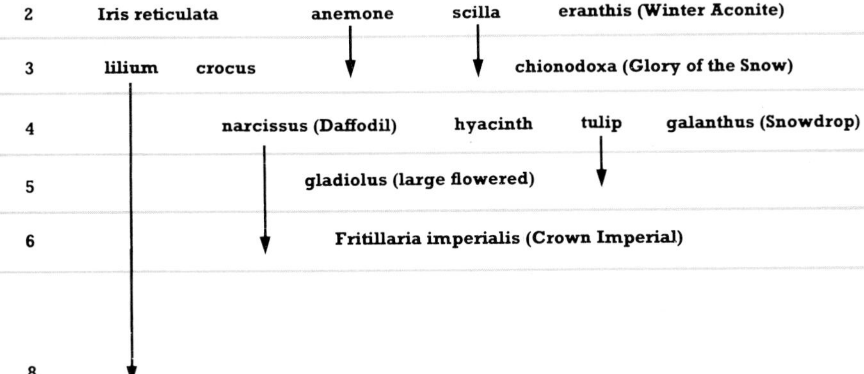

the house during the winter. These are planted up in early autumn and for house display I like to use ornamental bowls for the hyacinths and flower pots for the daffodils.

Bulbs planted in pots can be grown in a soil-based compost but for ornamental bowls without drainage holes I recommend using the special bulb fibre which can be bought and which will not go sour. Wet the fibre thoroughly, squeeze it out and place a layer in the bottom of the bowl. Set the bulbs on this, spacing them so that they do not touch and fill in around them with more fibre, leaving only the tips showing.

Below Planting daffodil bulbs in tiers enables twice the number to be put into a pot and increases the final effect

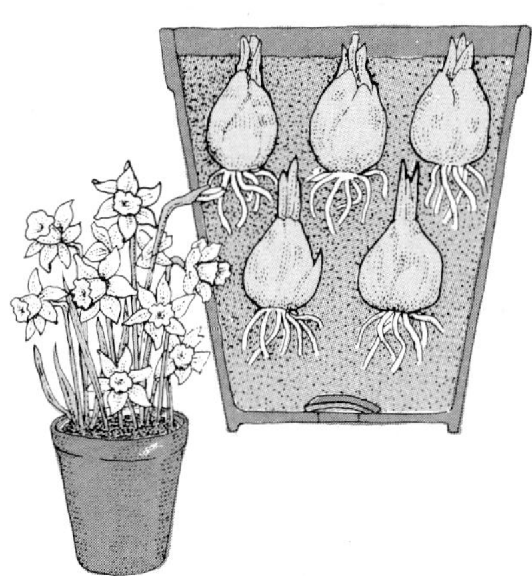

Helpful hint

When planting daffodils in pots I like to put the bulbs in two layers, with a layer of soil in between. The bulbs in the top layer are placed above the spaces between the bulbs in the bottom layer and in this way it is possible to grow more plants in the one pot.

After planting up, the pots or bowls must be placed in a cool, dark place indoors or stood outside and covered with several inches of peat. Here they should be left for 8 to 10 weeks to allow a good root system to develop. When brought into the light, they should still be kept in a cool place until the flowers show. Keep the compost or bulb fibre moist.

After flowering, the bulbs can be planted out in the garden to complete their growth and here they will flower in succeeding years.

Vegetables

Vegetables are interesting to grow and satisfying to eat. Try your luck with some of the easier crops and I'm sure you will be surprised at your success. Even in a small garden there may be a patch of ground which can be used for some tomatoes, runner beans, possibly a few lettuce. And, if not, why not follow the old style of cottage garden and plant them in the flower borders?

The three important basic requirements are:

1 A position in as much sun as possible.

2 Adequate feeding – use a general fertiliser several times during the growing season.

3 A good supply of water; mulching with organic matter or black polythene will help to keep the soil moist.

In many cases you will also have to provide netting to keep the birds away from the seeds and especially the young cabbage plants.

Methods of soil preparation and seed sowing have already been described, see pages 10 and 32. If you plan to grow such crops as beans, peas, lettuces, onions, radish or spinach, dig some organic matter into the soil in the autumn before sowing. Acid soils must be limed if the brassica crops are to be grown but there is no need to add in organic matter for these. For the root crops – beetroot, carrot, swede and turnips – sprinkle on a dressing of general fertiliser before sowing. Ideally, the position of each type of crop should be changed each year; this prevents a build up of disease in the soil and also makes allowance for the fact that crops take different amounts of plant nutrients from the soil. This is known as crop rotation.

The main vegetable crops fall into a number of categories depending on the cultural requirements:

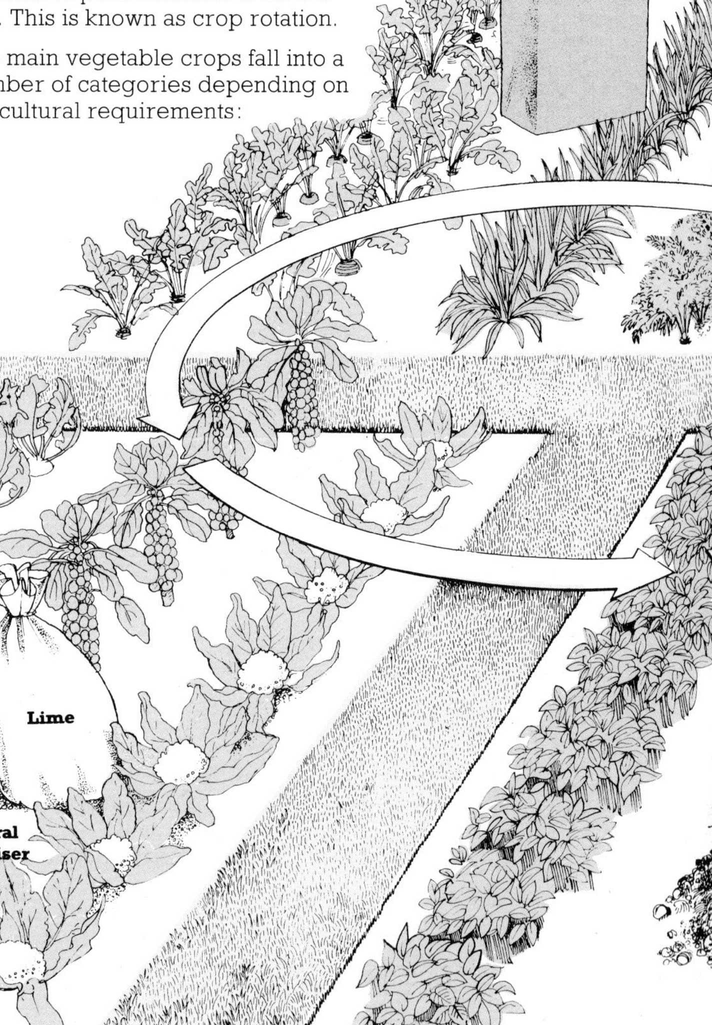

Crop Rotation. One area should be dressed with general fertiliser and used for root crops

The second area is dressed with general fertiliser and lime if necessary and used for the brassicas

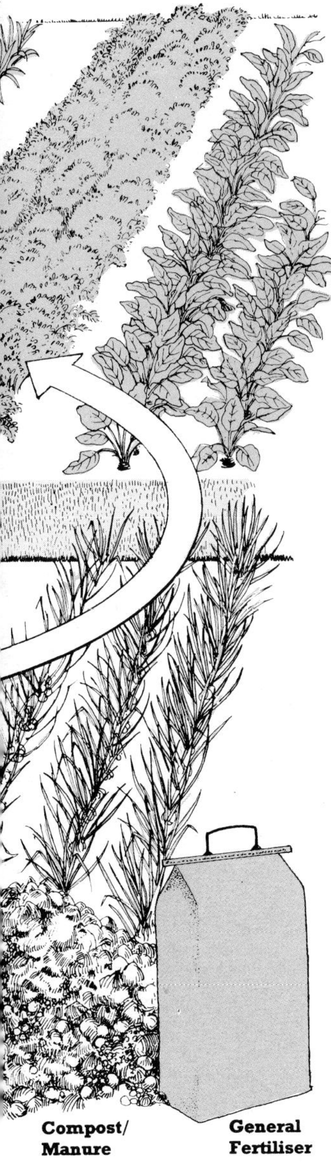

The leafy crops

Spinach spinach beet, lettuce.

Spinach beet or leaf beet is the easiest of these to grow and is very economical as the plants will crop for twelve months. Lettuce must be sown sparingly and frequently otherwise the crop is produced simultaneously and then bolts (the stem elongates preparatory to producing a seed head). All these require adequate supplies of nitrogen and should be fed occasionally with a general fertiliser.

The bulb crops

Onions, leeks, shallots.

Of these the onion is the best crop for the beginner to try. It can be produced from seed or 'sets'. The latter are small bulbs which grow to full size in the season. The bulb crops require rich soil and good watering.

The brassica crops

Cabbage, Chinese cabbage, broccoli, cauliflowers, Brussels sprouts, kale.

Not the easiest of crops to grow, their main needs are full sun, frequent watering and very well firmed soil. They are subject to attack from a range of pests and diseases.

The root crops

Beetroot, radish, carrots, parsnips, turnips, Jerusalem artichoke.

Success with these depends largely on the texture of the soil – a light well-drained soil is the best. Stoney or clayey soils do not give satisfactory results.

Third area dressed with compost and then fertiliser and used for the legumes, onions, lettuce, radish, and spinach

The legumes

Broad, French or runner beans, peas.

Of these, broad and runner beans are the best for the beginner – cropping well and giving a real sense of achievement. Keep the roots moist by mulching and feed regularly.

The vines

Marrows, including courgettes, pumpkins, melons, cucumbers.

All very tender crops which must not be sown or planted while there is danger of frost, even then the melons and frame cucumbers must have the protection of a frame. Ideally, organic matter must be added to the soil around each planting site. Courgettes are especially recommended as easy to grow and cropping well. Ridge cucumbers are the kind to choose for growing outside.

Potatoes

Soil containing organic matter is a basic requirement for a good crop. Potatoes are subject to attack from a range of pests and diseases and unless you have a lot of space I would recommend growing only early crops.

Tomatoes

These are raised from seed sown under glass for planting out in late May. Alternatively, buy young plants from the garden centre or other retailer, plant out in well manured soil or in growing bags. Water well and feed from the time flowers appear. The side shoots which grow from the angles between the leaves and main stem must be removed when they appear.

The easy vegetables

Spinach beet, runner and broad beans, lettuce, onions, beetroot, marrows (courgettes), and tomatoes would be my choice for a beginner.

Vegetables

Vegetables a sowing, planting and harvesting chart

	When to sow outdoors	When to sow under glass	When to plant	Depth to sow	Distance between rows	Distance to thin
Broad beans	Feb-Jun	Jan-Feb	Apr	5 cm (2 in)	60 cm (2 ft)	15 cm (6 in)
French beans	Apr-Jun	Jan-Feb		2·5 cm (1 in)	45 cm (1½ ft)	20 cm (8 in)
Runner beans	May-Jun	Apr	Jun	5 cm (2 in)	1·5 m (5 ft)	23 cm (9 in)
Beetroot	Mar-Jul			2·5 cm (1 in)	38 cm (15 in)	15 cm (6 in)
Leaf beet	Apr-Jul			2·5 cm (1 in)	45 cm (1½ ft)	23 cm (9 in)
Broccoli	Mar-May		Jun-Jul	1 cm (½ in)	60 cm (2 ft)	45 cm (1½ ft)
Brussels sprouts	Mar-Apr	Feb	Apr-Jun	1 cm (½ in)	75 cm (2½ ft)	75 cm (2½ ft)
Spring Cabbage	Jul-Aug		Sep-Oct	1 cm (½ in)	45 cm (1½ ft)	30 cm (1 ft)
Sum. & Aut. Cabbage	Mar-May	Jan-Feb	Jun-Jul	1 cm (½ in)	60 cm (2 ft)	60 cm (2 ft)
Winter Cabbage	May		Jun-Jul	1 cm (½ in)	60 cm (2 ft)	60 cm (2 ft)
Carrots	Mar-Jun			0·5 cm (¼ in)	30 cm (1 ft)	10 cm (4 in)
Summer Cauliflower	Sept	Jan-Feb	Apr	1 cm (½ in)	60 cm (2 ft)	45 cm (1½ ft)
Autumn & Winter Cauliflower	Apr-May		Jul	1 cm (½ in)	75 cm (2½ ft)	60 cm (2 ft)
Kale	Apr-May		Jul-Aug	1 cm (½ in)	60 cm (2 ft)	60 cm (2 ft)
Leeks	Mar	Jan-Feb	May-Jun	1 cm (½ in)	30 cm (1 ft)	23 cm (9 in)
Lettuce	Mar-Oct	Jan-Mar Sep-Oct		1 cm (½ in)	30 cm (1 ft)	23 cm (9 in)
Marrow	May	Apr	Late May	2·5 cm (1 in)	1 m (3 ft)	60 cm (2 ft)
Onions	Mar Aug-Sep	Jan	Mar-Apr	1 cm (½ in)	30 cm (1 ft)	15 cm (6 in)
Parsnips	Mar-May			2·5 cm (1 in)	45 cm (1½ ft)	20 cm (8 in)
Peas	Mar-Jun Oct	Jan-Feb		5 cm (2 in)	60 cm-1·5 m (2-5 ft)	8 cm (3 in)
Early Potatoes			Mar	13 cm (5 in)	60 cm (2 ft)	30 cm (1 ft)
Maincrop Potatoes			Apr	13 cm (5 in)	75 cm (2½ ft)	45 cm (1½ ft)
Radish	Mar-Aug	Feb		0·5 cm (¼ in)	23 cm (9 in)	1 cm (½ in)
Spinach	Mar-Sep			2·5 cm (1 in)	30 cm (1 ft)	15 cm (6 in)
Swede	May-Jun			1 cm (½ in)	30 cm (1 ft)	20 cm (8 in)
Turnip	Mar-Sep			1 cm (½ in)	30 cm (1 ft)	15 cm (6 in)

Harvest	Cultivation hints	
Jun-Oct	Autumn sowing possible in sheltered areas. Pinch out shoot tips when beans form.	Broad beans
May-Sep	Not frost hardy – do not sow too early outside. Harvest when they are a usable size.	French beans
Jul-Oct	Not frost hardy. Stake securely. Pick regularly to keep plants cropping.	Runner beans
Jul-Oct	For early use choose globe varieties, long-rooted kinds for late crops and storing.	Beetroot
Jul-Mar	Includes perpetual spinach and Swiss chard. Sow in succession to maintain supply.	Leaf beet
Sep-Jun	Sow and plant in very well-firmed soil, keep watered. Pick when flower shoots form.	Broccoli
Sep-Feb	Plant firmly, feed occasionally, water well. Pick sprouts from bottom of stem upwards.	Brussels sprouts
Apr-Jun	Plant firmly. Keep a watch for caterpillars and other pests and for club root disease. Good varieties: April, Wheeler's Imperial, Offenham.	Spring Cabbage
Jul-Oct	Plant firmly. Keep a watch for pests and diseases. Good varieties: Greyhound, Hispi, Winnigstadt, Autumn Supreme, Market Topper.	Sum. & Aut. Cabbage
Oct-Jan	Plant firmly. Keep a watch for pests and diseases. Good varieties: Winter White, Christmas Drumhead.	Winter Cabbage
Jun-Oct	Sow thinly. Use stump-rooted kinds for early sowings, long-rooted kinds for storing.	Carrots
Jun-Jul	Plant firmly. Water well. Bend inner leaves over the curd. Cut when separate sections of the curd can be seen. Good varieties: Snowball, Flora Blanca, Barrier Reef.	Summer Cauliflower
Aug-Jun	Plant firmly. Check after frost and firm in any which have been lifted. Bend inner leaves over the curd. Cut when separate sections of curd can be seen. Good varieties: Snow's Winter White, Walcheren, St. George, Late Queen.	Autumn & Winter Cauliflower
Nov-May	Withstands cold weather. Plant firmly. Cut the leaves or shoots as required.	Kale
Sep-May	Well fertilised soil. Plant in 15-cm (6-in) deep holes and water well.	Leeks
all year	Choose varieties to give year-round supply and sow little and often. Water well, feed occasionally. Pull when the heart is firm to the touch.	Lettuce
Jul-Sep	Courgettes are a type of bush marrow. Sunny position and rich soil are needed. Feed and water well.	Marrow
Feb-Oct	Sunny site and well prepared soil. Bend over the tops when growth slows down.	Onions
Sept-Mar	Sow seeds in groups of 2 or 3 and then thin to leave the strongest seedling.	Parsnips
Jun-Oct	Deeply dug, well manured soil required. Water well and provide some form of support. Pick as soon as the pods are well filled.	Peas
Jun-Jul	Sprout potatoes by keeping in a light frost-free place until shoots show. After planting earth up regularly once the shoots appear. Harvest when plants flower.	Early Potatoes
Aug-Oct	The treatment of maincrop potatoes is the same as for early potatoes. See above for cultivation hints.	Maincrop Potatoes
Apr-Oct	Need a rich moist soil as this crop must be grown fast. Pull frequently.	Radish
all year	Choose varieties to give year-round supply. Pick continually taking outer leaves.	Spinach
Oct-Mar	Well cultivated soil. Water well. Lift from Oct.; remainder in Dec. for storing.	Swede
Jun-Mar	Needs good soil for fast growth. Water well. Harvest when the size of a cricket ball.	Turnip

Pests, diseases and weeds

I was always taught that when it comes to dealing with pests and diseases, prevention is better than cure. Keep an eye on all the plants in the garden – an early diagnosis and swift treatment make most pests and diseases easier to control. For example, a spray in the early part of the year against greenfly on roses or blackfly on broad beans often means that there will be little need to spray during the rest of the summer – a saving of both time and money. This is because these insects increase rapidly once they get a hold and you stand a better chance of controlling them in the early stages when they are not likely to be around in such quantities.

This is even more important with fungus diseases such as mildew and blackspot. A spray when the first sign of trouble is noticed will do much to prevent the diseases affecting the foliage so badly that they never recover from them throughout the season.

Here I would like to put in a word of warning on the use of chemicals: many of these remedies are poisonous and must be handled with care. Although I have not recommended any of the highly poisonous ones here, it should be remembered that most are capable of doing some damage. When handling chemicals be safe not sorry:

1 Always read and follow the manufacturer's instructions.

2 Wash off accidental splashes straight away and always wash after using sprays.

3 Do not inhale the vapour.

4 Keep containers well stoppered and labelled and locked up out of the reach of children's hands.

5 All used containers should be put in refuse bins, if metal (but not aerosol) they should be punctured and glass ones broken and wrapped well in newspaper.

6 Keep the spray equipment for this purpose only and wash it well.

7 Observe the periods of time which must be allowed to elapse between applications of chemicals and the harvesting of crops.

8 When spraying open flowers, do so in the evening when there is less danger of bees being affected.

9 Do not attempt to spray when there is a breeze blowing which may waft the droplets around.

The chemicals available

There are a bewildering variety of chemical sprays but many contain the same active ingredient and differ slightly in their formulation and their trade names. When it comes to the way in which they work, they are divided into two main groups, the systemic and the non-systemic.

The systemic pesticides and fungicides are absorbed through the leaves and stems of the plant into the sap and here they remain effective for several weeks. Fungal diseases growing through the plant cells or insects feeding on the plants will be affected.

Non-systemic pesticides and fungicides stay on the surface of the plant and affect the insect or fungus by direct contact on them or by poisoning the outside of the plant. These do not remain effective for very long and the dose must be repeated.

The insecticides

Carbaryl Sold as Carbaryl, Murvin, Sevin or Wormkiller.
CONTROLS codling moth, caterpillars, pea moth, earthworms, leatherjackets.
Harmful to bees and fish.

Derris Sold as Derris.
CONTROLS aphids, caterpillars, red spider mites, gooseberry sawfly, raspberry beetle. Harmful to fish.

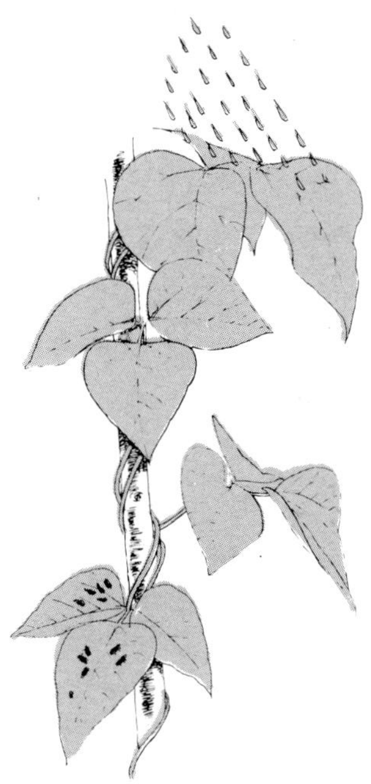

Systemic insecticides and fungicides are carried around in the sap and will affect pests and diseases on any part of the plant

A non-systemic chemical only kills pests if it falls directly on them or if it poisons the feeding surfaces

Dimethoate Sold as Dimethoate, Systemic Insecticide or Rogor E.
CONTROLS aphids, red spider mites, sawflies.
Harmful to bees, fish, livestock, birds and animals.

Gamma-HCH Sold as Gamma BHC, Lindane, Sybol.
CONTROLS aphids, cabbage root fly, sawflies, woolly aphid, caterpillars, tortrix moth.
Harmful to bees, fish and livestock.
Do not use on cucumbers, melons, marrows, hydrangeas, vines or young tomato plants.

Malathion Sold as Malathion or in mixtures.
CONTROLS most insect pests.
Harmful to bees and fish.
Do not use on ferns, sweet peas, crassulas.

Pirimiphos-methyl Sold as Keri-spray (includes pyrethrins), Pest-killer.
CONTROLS most insects on house-plants (including white fly and red spider).
Dangerous to bees and harmful to fish.

Pyrethrin Sold as Plant Pest Killer. Anti-Ant Powder, Coopers Insect Powder.
CONTROLS most insects. This is one of the safest insecticides.

Tar oil Sold as Tar Oil Winter Wash, Mortegg.
CONTROLS overwintering stages of aphids, scale insects, mealy bugs, tortrix moth and others.
Harmful to fish.

The fungicides

Benomyl Systemic fungicide sold as Benlate.
CONTROLS leaf spots, mildews, botrytis.

Bupirimate Sold as Nimrod.
CONTROLS black spot, mildew.

Captan Sold as Captan, Orthocide.
CONTROLS black spot, botrytis, scab, damping off.
Harmful to fish.

Lime sulphur
CONTROLS leaf curl, powdery mildew on fruit.

Mercurous chloride Sold as Calomel, Cyclosan, also mixed with another chemical to make Lawn Sand.
CONTROLS club root and other diseases as well as cabbage root fly.
Harmful to fish.

Thiram Sold as Thiram, General Fungicide.
CONTROLS botrytis, downy mildew, rusts, black spot.

Zineb Sold as Zineb, Dithane.
CONTROLS blight, mildew, leaf spot, rust.

Never mix chemicals together unless recommended to do so on the bottle or packet. Several fungicides and insecticides are compatible but manufacturer's suggestions must be followed. I always mix up an insecticide and add a compatible fungicide to it to make a combined spray. This saves doing the job twice and seems to be more effective than buying a ready mixed combined fungicide and insecticide.

Spraying equipment

There is a big range of spray equipment for sale. Choose a size which will do the job you require of it and a nozzle which will give you a fine but forceful spray pattern and good coverage over stems, leaves and buds.

Remember that unused spray solution cannot be kept and don't mix up more than you need.

Spray only the plants suffering from pest or disease attack – don't get spray happy and spread it all round the garden.

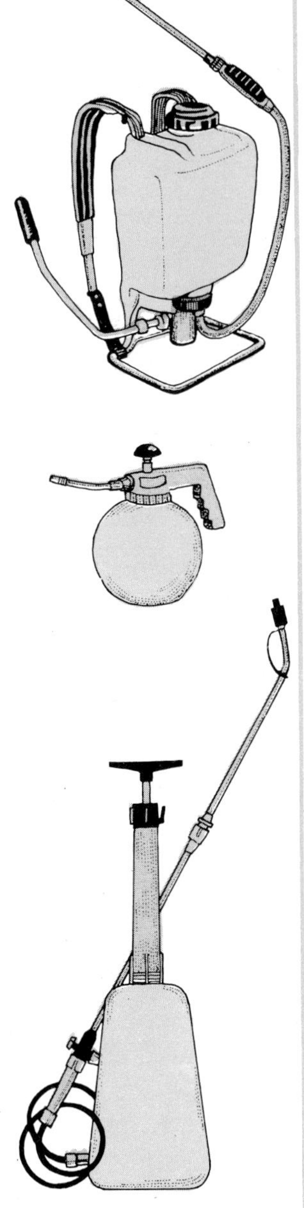

A selection of sprayers

Pests, diseases and weeds

Insect friends

Many of the familiar insects and small animals seen in the garden are not harmful to the plants; on the contrary, they are the natural predators of some of the plant pests and it is to safeguard these and also the bees that I advise taking great care in the use of pesticides. Ladybirds, spiders, many beetles, centipedes, even to a certain extent earwigs, should all be welcomed. As a general rule, any insect that moves fast can be regarded as a friend.

Keeping down attacks of pests and diseases

Good gardening methods will do much to keep plants trouble free.

1 Keep the garden as weed free as possible and pick up fallen fruit, leaves, etc.

2 Burn diseased plants as quickly as possible.

3 Watch out for the first signs of pest and disease attack and take prompt action.

4 Water plants properly. Feed when necessary – plants that are growing well are less likely to be attacked.

5 Replace plants which show the same disease symptoms year after year. This is particularly apparent on roses.

6 Give plants the right growing conditions.

The pests

Aphids Small, soft-skinned insects commonly known as greenfly and blackfly which suck the plant sap. Can attack all plants.
DAMAGE Leaves distorted, vigour reduced, substance (honeydew) secreted which encourages a black fungal growth called sooty mould.
CONTROL Spray with dimethoate, malathion, pirimiphos-methyl, derris or menazon. Pinch out the tips of broad beans when the pods have formed.

Spray fruit trees in winter with a tar oil winter wash to kill overwintering eggs.

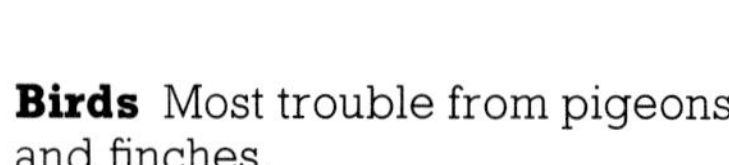

Birds Most trouble from pigeons and finches.
DAMAGE Eat newly sown seed, nip out developing fruit buds, eat young vegetable crops especially cabbages and their relatives and damage young flowers.
CONTROL Use bird repellents on seed and buds, cottoning over flowers. Only sure method is to use protective netting.

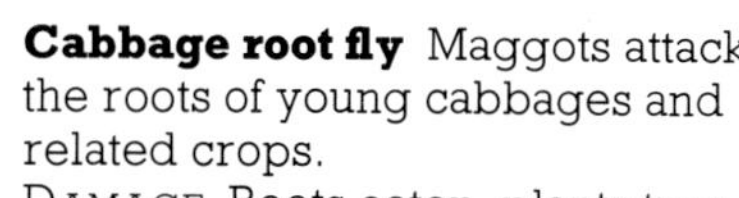

Cabbage root fly Maggots attack the roots of young cabbages and related crops.
DAMAGE Roots eaten, plants turn bluish, stunted growth.
CONTROL Dust seedlings with 4 per cent calomel dust. Dust seed-beds with gamma HCH or pirimiphos-methyl.

Carrot fly It is the maggot stage which causes the damage. Attacks carrots and parsnips.
DAMAGE Leaves wilt, maggots tunnel in the roots.
CONTROL Dust soil around seedlings with naphthalene or gamma HCH. The flies are attracted by the smell of the foliage at thinning time, so sow sparsely to avoid the need for thinning.

Caterpillars The larvae of butterflies and moths. In the garden expect most trouble on cabbages and related crops.
DAMAGE Irregular holes in the leaves.
CONTROL Hand pick. Spray with derris, HCH or malathion.

Codling moth Attacks apples and pears. White grub found in the fruit in late summer.
CONTROL Spray with malathion after petal fall, spray twice more at fortnightly intervals. Spray with tar oil wash in winter.

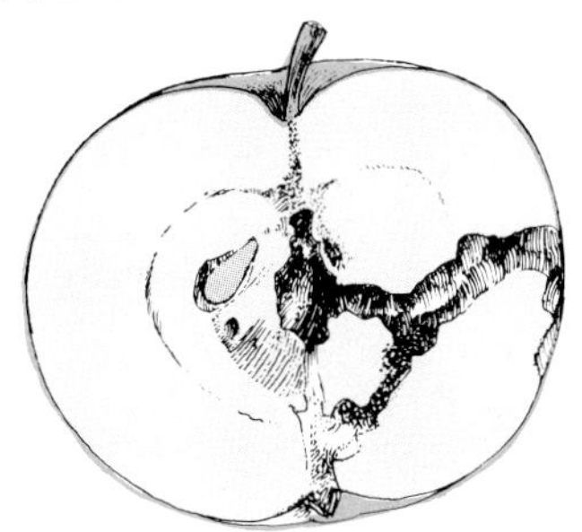

Cuckoo spit Mass of frothy liquid on young shoots, harbours small sap-sucking insect. Attacks many garden plants.
DAMAGE Similar to that of aphids.
CONTROL Hand pick, spray with HCH, malathion, dimethoate.

Flea beetle Beetles eat holes in leaves of turnips and most green vegetables. May destroy seedlings.
CONTROL Occasional dusting at seedling stage with derris or gamma HCH.

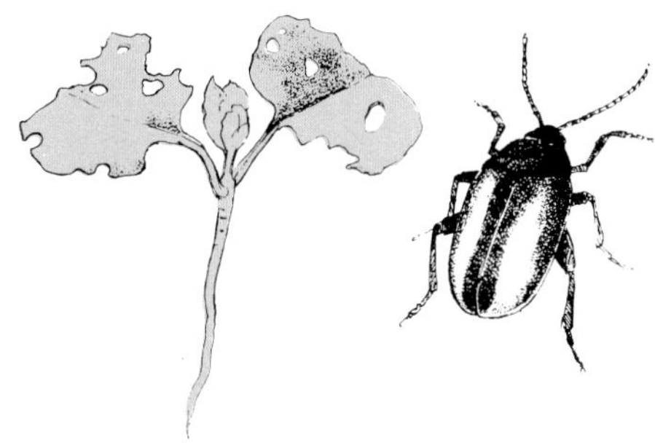

Leaf-miners Maggots of several kinds of flies. Attack celery, chrysanthemums, cineraria, hollies, lilacs.
DAMAGE White lines or blisters on the leaves.
CONTROL Pick off and burn infected leaves. Spray with HCH, malathion.

Pests, diseases and weeds

Leatherjackets The larvae of the daddy-long-legs which live in soil and attack many plants including grass.
Damage Roots eaten.
Control Apply carbaryl or HCH to the soil or apply in liquid form on lawns.

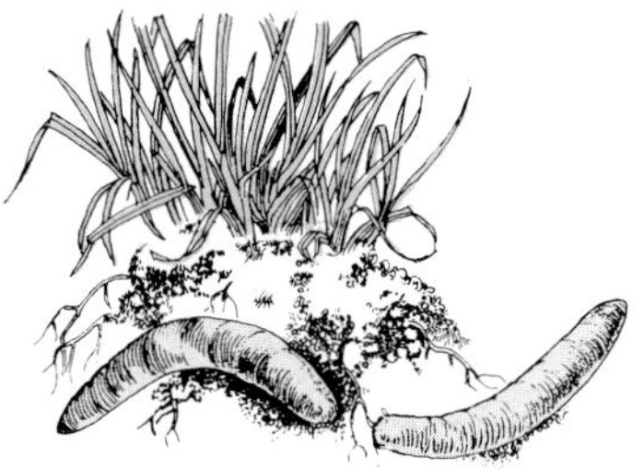

Mealy bug Attacks vines, peaches, apricots, cacti and other greenhouse plants. The small insect is protected by a coating of white wax.
Damage Sucks the sap and weakens growth, leaves turn yellow.
Control Touch each bug with a paint brush soaked in methylated spirit. Spray with malathion, dimethoate, or petroleum oil.

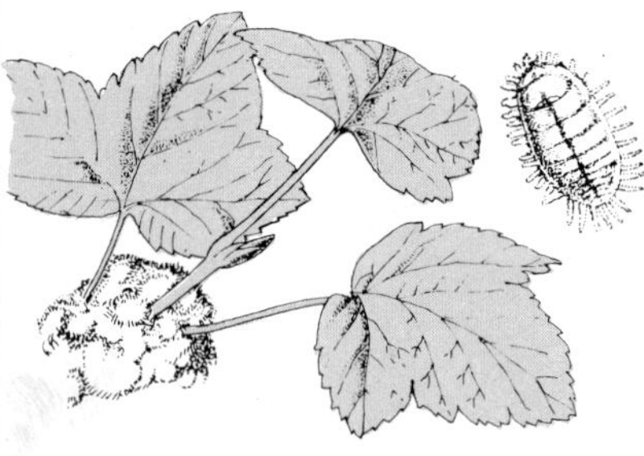

Pea moth The caterpillar feeds on the peas inside the pods.
Damage Maggoty peas.
Control Spray with carbaryl in the evening at flowering time.

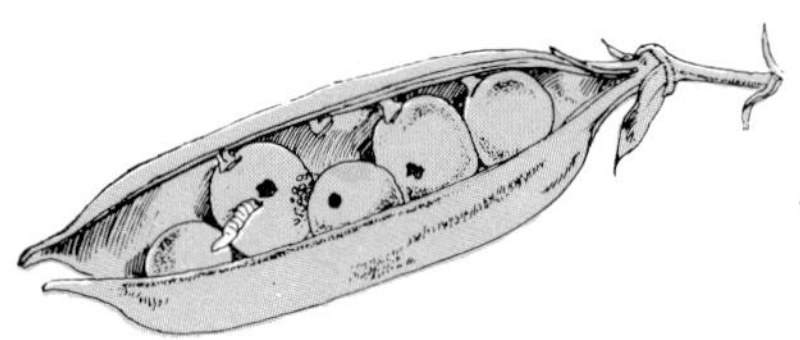

Red spider mite Almost microscopic mites which attack many plants. Found mainly under glass, and on apple trees in Britain.
Damage Sucks sap, leaves become mottled and fall, fine webbing on the underside.
Control Spray with malathion. As these mites thrive in a hot, dry atmosphere, spray the foliage and keep atmosphere damp.

Sawfly The caterpillars of several kinds of sawfly attack most fruit.
Damage Gooseberry leaves eaten, apple and plum fruits contain maggots, gummy exudate produced.
Control Spray gooseberries with malathion or derris. Apple and plums with dimethoate one week after petal fall.

Scale insect Several kinds of sucking insect. Attack many plants, both outdoors and under glass. Protected by a waxy, shell-like secretion. Look like small limpets.
Damage Sucks sap, the sticky substance secreted by the insect encourages a black fungal growth called sooty mould.
Control Spray with malathion or a systemic insecticide. Use a tar oil spray on trees in winter.

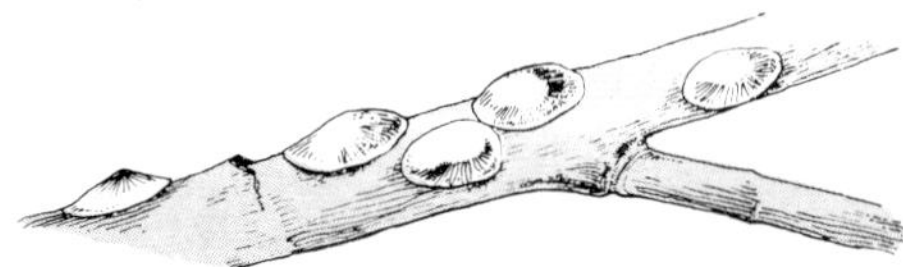

Slugs and snails Attack most garden plants.
DAMAGE Leaves, flowers, stem bases eaten.
CONTROL Poisoned baits or pellets placed under a tile, out of reach of children, animals and birds.

Tortrix moth Attacks apples.
DAMAGE Larvae eat leaves and surface of fruit. Leaves may be spun together to contain the larvae or a leaf stuck to the damaged part of the fruit.
CONTROL Spray with tar oil wash in winter or gamma HCH later in the season.

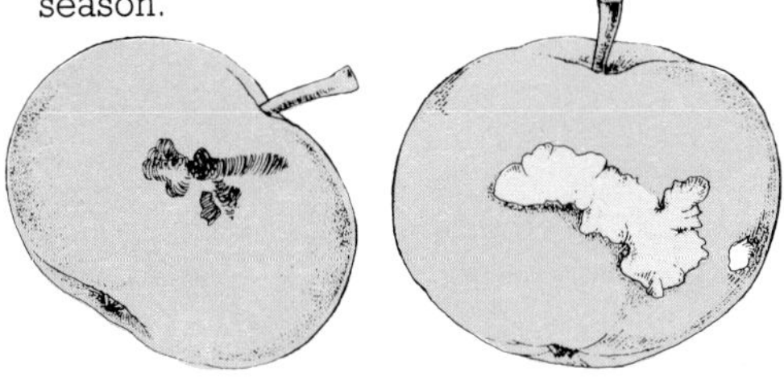

White fly Small moth-like insects found clinging to underside of leaves which fly up when disturbed. Found mostly under glass, but one kind attacks cabbages.
DAMAGE Caused by the scale-like larvae which suck sap and produce a sticky excrement which is followed by sooty mould.
CONTROL Spray with malathion or pirimiphos-methyl.

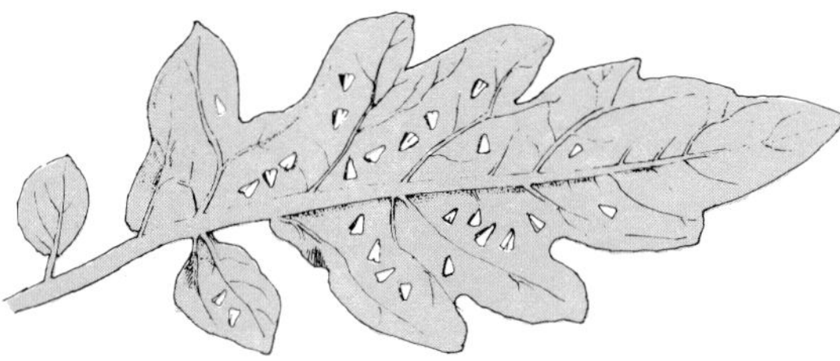

Diseases and troubles

Black spot Circular black spots on the upper surface of rose leaves. Defoliation may result.
CONTROL Spray with a systemic fungicide or bupirimate. Some varieties are immune.

Blossom-end rot This affects tomatoes, the fruits develop black patches at the ends opposite the stalks.
CAUSE Insufficient and erratic watering. The symptoms may not appear until several weeks after the irregular watering occurred.

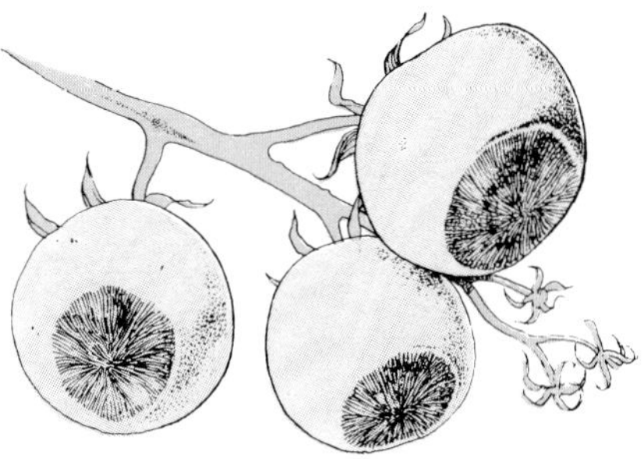

Blotchy ripening Tomato fruits marked with hard green or yellow areas.
CONTROL Grow in well fertilised soil. Give an added dressing of sulphate of potash.

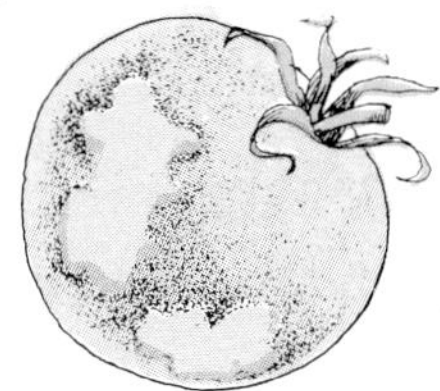

Pests, diseases and weeds

Botrytis Fungus which attacks a wide range of plants, especially important on lettuce and strawberries.
SYMPTOMS Grey velvety growth, blackened tissues, plants may keel over and rot.
CONTROL Improve air circulation by not planting too closely. Spray with benomyl or systemic fungicide.

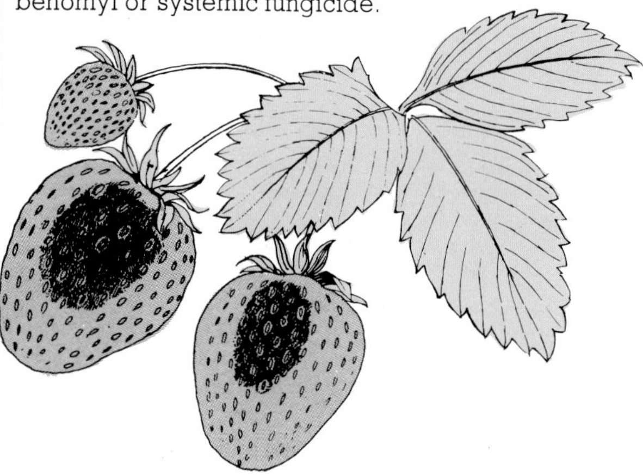

Club root Fungus disease which attacks the roots of cabbages and related crops. Only likely to be a problem on acid soils.
SYMPTOMS Wilting and blueing of the foliage. Infected plants will have swollen and misshapen roots.
CONTROL Dress acid soil with hydrated lime. Dust calomel along the rows at planting time.

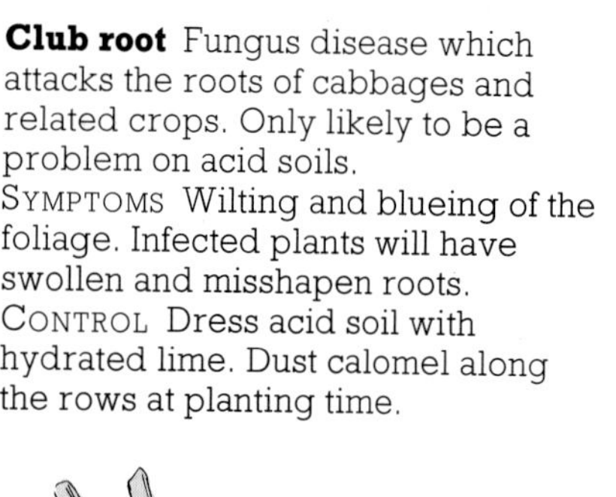

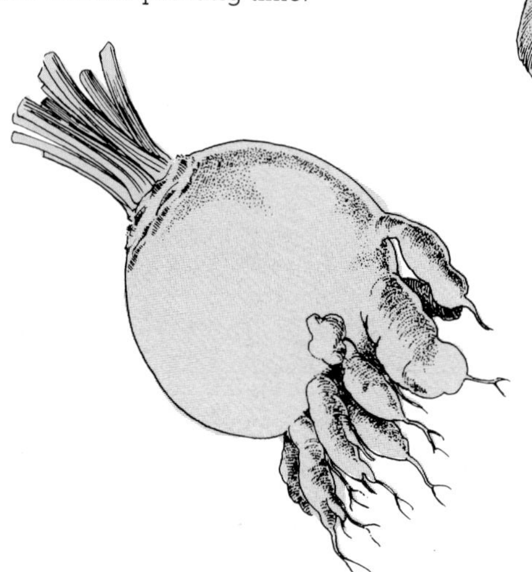

Damping off Fungus disease affecting a wide range of seedlings.
SYMPTOMS The fungus attacks the stems at soil level and, as a result, the seedlings keel over.
CONTROL Try to prevent by sowing thinly, keep seedlings in good light, use sterilised seed sowing compost. Once disease has developed, water with Cheshunt Compound.

Leaf curl A common disease of peaches and nectarines.
SYMPTOMS Leaves become curled and puckered and develop bright red blisters. Vigour of the plant reduced.
CONTROL Spray with captan or lime sulphur in February when the buds begin to swell. Repeat in autumn when the leaves are falling.

Mildew Many types of mildew affecting a wide range of crops. Very noticeable in some varieties of rose.
SYMPTOMS White powdery mould on stems, leaves and blossom. It is likely to be worse in damp weather.
CONTROL Spray with a systemic fungicide or with thiram bupirimate or zineb fortnightly.

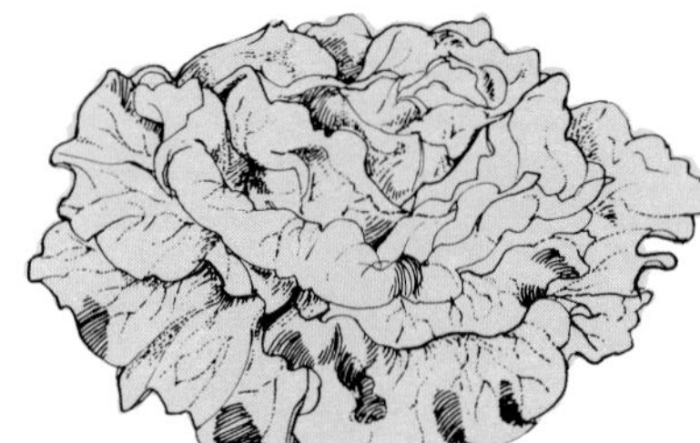

Rust Caused by several different fungi and appearing on a range of plants. Most noticeable on roses, hollyhocks and antirrhinums.
SYMPTOMS Small orange or rust-coloured spots on the leaves.
CONTROL Spray regularly with thiram or zineb.

Virus A wide range of disease-causing organisms which attack many crops.
SYMPTOMS Many and varied: mottled, distorted leaves, stunted growth, deformed or oddly coloured flowers.
CONTROL Dig up and burn infected plants. Plant virus-free stock if this is available. Keep down aphids and other sap-sucking insects which spread the disease.

Weeding and the use of weed-killers

Weeds in the garden can be dealt with by hoeing or hand weeding or, in some instances, by the use of chemicals which are known as weedkillers or herbicides. A number of rules should accompany their application.

1 Always weed vegetables and fruit crops with a hoe or hand tool. (See tools, p40.)

2 Plants growing closely together should always be hand weeded.

3 Apply weedkillers by means of a rose or sprinkle bar attachment to the watering can. Wash all equipment well after use. Use on a still day.

Contact weedkillers These kill the parts of the plant with which they come into contact. Some, such as sodium chlorate, can be carried about in the soil water and may kill plants well away from the point of application as well as remaining active for several months. Sodium chlorate is only recommended for use on paths and paving and must be applied with care. It is inflammable.

Paraquat is a more useful contact herbicide as it is inactivated by the soil but kills all leaves and young stems with which it comes into contact.

Selective weedkillers Mostly used for killing weeds on lawns (see p29). They are particularly effective in spring.

The most common ones contain MCPA, mecoprop or 2,4-D.

Residual weedkillers Chemicals which remain near the soil surface and kill the seedling weeds as they grow. Can be used on paths and also between roses, shrubs and fruit trees.

Dichlobenil and simazine are examples of these.

Index

Index

Abbreviation: d = line drawing

Index

Index